PRACTICAL
PROCEDURI

FOURTH EDITION

John Harrison

LONGMAN

Addison Wesley Longman
Addison Wesley Longman Limited,
Edinburgh Gate, Harlow,
Essex CM20 2JE, England
and associated companies throughout the world

First published 1984
Fourth edition 1996

British Library Cataloguing in Publication Data
A catalogue entry for this title is available from the
British Library

ISBN 0–582–29334–0

Library of Congress Cataloging-in-Publication Data
A catalog entry for this title is available from the
Library of Congress

Typeset by 36 in New Baskerville
Printed in Great Britain by Henry Ling Ltd., at the
Dorset Press, Dorchester, Dorset.

Contents

Preface

Practical Office Procedures is in three parts:

1 Case studies involving three office workers, their places of employment and their leisure activities, together with a scenario for an office procedures examination.
2 Assignments, most of which are associated with the case studies but several in each unit have been taken from the Pitman Qualifications (PQ), formerly PEI, examinations in Office Procedures Levels 1 and 2.
3 Specimen master forms which can be copied for use in the assignments.

The assignments are set at an appropriate level for students preparing for Office Procedures awards: NVQ Levels 1 and 2; GNVQ Intermediate; Pitman Qualifications Levels 1 and 2; and GCSE Business Studies.

Each unit contains:

● a full range of realistic tasks for use in class or at home without the need for specialist equipment;
● tasks for completion by computer or word processor;
● tasks for completion at work in the various departments of an organisation;
● the recommended NVQ performance criteria to assess the standards required for competence in the tasks.

The fourth edition of this book has been brought into line with the latest NVQ criteria for Levels 1 and 2 Administration Awards and it has been fully updated with the latest office services and procedures. There are new units in work planning and scheduling; travel arrangements; and organising meetings and other events.

There is no doubt that student activities are most effective when realistic business situations are simulated and actual forms and business documents used in a realistic learning situation. For this reason a comprehensive bank of master forms specially designed for the assignments has been supplied in Section E to assist in creating realistic materials for students to use.

The case studies and scenario, set at the appropriate level of experience and background for new entrants to an office, should help to create an effective and stimulating setting for the assignments. The office activities of the community association are intended to link the study of office procedures with students' leisure-time pursuits and so draw attention to the relevance and importance of office skills and administration in all walks of life.

The essential background knowledge and related progress checks in the form of multiple choice and short answer questions for each of the units in this book are given in the accompanying textbook *Office Procedures*.

I hope that the experience students gain from working through the assignments in *Practical Office Procedures* will be enjoyable and rewarding and, at the same time, help them to gain the necessary competences in the tasks and a better understanding and knowledge of office practice and procedures.

JH

Acknowledgements

The author and publishers wish to thank the following for permission to reproduce forms and other documents:

Alliance & Leicester Giro
Mrs Valerie Bell of Eastleigh College
Midland Bank plc
Parcelforce
Royal Mail
The Sunday Telegraph
Her Majesty's Theatre
Crown copyright material is reproduced with the permission of the Controller of Her Majesty's Stationery Office.

The performance criteria and competences featured in this book are reproduced by kind permission of the Administration Lead Body.

We are also grateful to Pitman Qualifications (formerly Pitman Examinations Institute) for permission to reproduce questions set in their examinations referred to as PQ OP1 (Office Procedures Level 1) and PQ OP2 (Office Procedures Level 2).

Assessment chart

Practical Office Procedures Unit		NVQ Level 1 Element	NVQ Level 2 Element	PQ OP1 Sec	PQ OP2 Sec
1	The role and relationship of office workers in the organisation	4.1	4.1	1	1
2	Buying and selling	–	7.2 10.1	3	4
3	Stock control	9.1/2	9.1/2	3	4
4	Receipts and payments	–	7.2 10.2	3	4
5	Petty cash	5.3	10.2	3	–
6	Wages and salaries	–	7.2	–	–
7	Filing	6.1/2	5.1/2	4	5
8	Incoming and outgoing mail	8.1/2	8.2	3/5	1
9	Work planning and scheduling	1.1/3	1.1/3 3.1/2	–	–
10	Computer systems and terminology	7.1	6.1/3	5	3
11	Reprography	7.2 3.1/2	3.3	5	3
12	Calculators	5.3	–	–	–
13	Health and safety	2.1/2	2.1	1	1
14	Oral communications	5.1/2	8.1	2	2
15	Written communication	5.2	7.1/2 8.1	2	2
16	Mail services	8.1/2	8.2	3	1
17	Receiving and assisting visitors	4.2 2.3	4.2 2.2	2	2
18	Travel arrangements	–	11.1/2	–	6
19	Organising meetings and other events	–	12.1/3	–	6
20	Sources of information	5.2/3	5.2	–	5

List of master forms for assignments

Case studies

Many of the activities in this book relate to the work experience of three office workers – Sarah Bates, Amanda Jackson and Paul Grant – as well as to the wider aspects of office work in their organisations and of their leisure-time activities. They left the Twyford Comprehensive School a year ago but have continued to keep in touch with each other at the Compton Community Association (CCA) in the evenings and at weekends. The Association is a flourishing organisation with its own premises in Twyford.

Amanda Jackson's father is the Chairman of the Association and she is the Assistant Secretary. The Association, which is a voluntary organisation open to people of all ages, aims to provide a wide range of social, cultural and sporting activities to cater for the needs of the local community. The CCA also provides the venue for community education classes in conjunction with the local College. The CCA's organisational structure is given in Fig 1.

- Sarah Bates works as a receptionist/telephonist at a firm of solicitors in the town – R W Fothergill & Co
- Paul Grant is an administrative trainee on a Youth Training Scheme and is attached to the Education Department of Westshire County Council
- Amanda Jackson is employed as a data entry clerk in the buying department of a firm of office furniture manufacturers – Systems Furniture plc

▶ R W FOTHERGILL & CO

Solicitors

R W Fothergill & Co is a well established and reputable firm of solicitors in the town centre of Twyford. It employs 16 full-time staff (as shown in the organisation chart in Fig 2) and several part-time secretarial staff as the need arises. The firm offers all the usual legal profes-sional services as well as serving as agents for one of the well known national insurance companies.

Sarah Bates, their receptionist/telephonist, joined the firm a year ago, and she is responsible to Mrs P Sherwin, the senior partner's private secretary. Sarah's position in the firm brings her into personal contact with clients when they telephone or call into the office and she enjoys this opportunity of being of service to them.

In addition to her duties as receptionist/telephonist, Sarah is responsible for issuing, ordering and keeping records of stationery. A stock record card is used for each item and once a year stocktaking takes place and a stock list is completed. Figure 3 is an extract from the stock list at 1 January 19– which you will need to refer to in carrying out some of the tasks.

▶ SYSTEMS FURNITURE plc

Office furniture manufacturers

Systems Furniture plc is engaged in the manufacture, distribution and sale of office furniture. It caters for the complete requirements of an organisation, including reception areas, mailrooms, general administration, secretarial, conference and lecture rooms, boardrooms and drawing offices. With the recent explosion in the use of screen-based information systems demand has increased considerably for furniture that is 'tailor-made' to accommodate the new technological systems. As a result, Systems Furniture plc has benefited from this demand and expanded rapidly.

The company has recently moved from London to the new Brookfield Industrial Estate in Twyford where it has larger premises to cater for the increased business. The names of the staff with their areas of responsibility are given on pages xv and xvi.

Fig 1 Compton Community Association

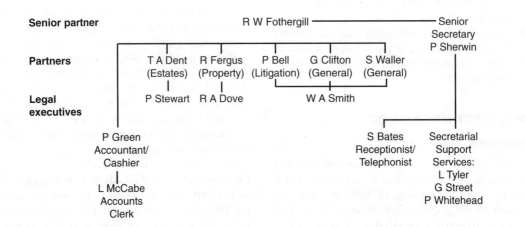

Fig 2 Organisation chart for R W Fothergill & Co

STOCK OF STATIONERY AT 1 JANUARY 19—								
Ref No	Item	Location	Unit size	Maximum	Re-order Level	Minimum	Balance in stock	Cost per unit
								£
100	Headed bond paper A4	A1	ream	50	20	10	25	5.00
101	Headed bond paper A5	A2	ream	50	20	10	44	4.00
102	Plain bond paper A3	A3	ream	30	10	5	12	4.50
103	Plain bond paper A4	A4	ream	60	20	10	52	4.00
104	Plain bond paper A5	A5	ream	50	20	10	28	4.00
105	Bank paper A3	A6	ream	30	10	5	28	4.00
106	Bank paper A4	A7	ream	60	20	10	54	3.75
107	Bank paper A5	A8	ream	50	20	10	18	3.50
108	Memo forms A4	A9	ream	20	6	4	10	4.00
109	Memo forms A5	A10	ream	20	6	4	14	3.75
110	Postcards	A11	50 pkt	20	6	4	12	2.50
111	Compliment slips	A12	50 pkt	20	8	6	12	3.50
112	Envelopes C3	B1	25 pkt	10	5	3	8	3.00
113	Envelopes C4	B2	25 pkt	20	6	4	14	2.50
114	Envelopes C5	B3	25 pkt	30	10	5	20	2.25
115	Envelopes C6	B4	25 pkt	40	12	8	38	2.00

Fig 3 Stock list

SYSTEMS FURNITURE plc

Directors
R A Lawes *Chairman and Managing Director*
C Haines
G A Woodhouse
P Gray

Executives
R P Lodge *Chief accountant*
P T Watkins *Chief cashier*
W Morris *Company secretary*
P Shearing *Marketing manager*
L A Scott *Home sales manager*
R Williams *Export sales manager*
C Bright *Advertising manager*
R N Young *Transport manager*
K Pratt *Office manager*
P Ridley *Chief buyer*
R Mitchell *Buyer*
N T Benney *Personnel manager*
P S Adams *Employment and training manager*
R Weller *Production manager*
P A Johns *Chief designer*

Supervisors
A Johnson *Accounting staff*
R Fisher *Secretarial services*

P A Bloom *Sales staff*
K Ash *Buying staff*
B T Mills *Production staff*
P Anderson *Safety officer*

Office staff
A T Palliser *Ledger clerk*
R O'Brien *Ledger clerk*
P Prince *Wages clerk*
N Tilling *Cashier*
M Beaver *Cost clerk*
T A Redpath *Credit control clerk*
J Wilkinson *Receptionist*
P Patel *Telephonist/telex operator*
R M Inge *Filing clerk*
G Attwood *Mailing clerk*
C Vaughan *Computer operator*
R Faulkner *Invoice clerk*
C Green *Invoice clerk*
P Jasper *Transport clerk*
P Griffith *Sales representative*
A Johnson *Sales representative*
C Lake *Sales representative*
P Ackroyd *Order clerk*
C Wilson *Stock control clerk*
R Page *Despatch clerk*

A Pearce *Production control clerk*
R A Mason *Secretary to managing director*
P Ellis *Secretary* ⎫ *Secretarial*
G Allan *Secretary* ⎬ *support*
T A Green *Secretary* ⎭ *service*
A Jackson *Data entry clerk – buying*
P R Richardson *Data entry clerk – sales*
R Southern *Data entry clerk – accounts*
G A Lucas *Data entry clerk – personnel*
N Aspinall *Data entry clerk– production*

Amanda Jackson works as a data entry clerk in the Buying Department and is responsible to Mr K Ash, the Buying Staff Supervisor.

Company data:
Bankers: Midland Bank plc, Twyford
Bank code: 40-19-48
Account No: 21357603
Girobank Account No: 6 143 2169

VAT Registration No: 3027560 21
Telephone No: 0193 384192
Telex No: 342689
Fax No: 0193 219673

Figures 4 and 5 are extracts from the company's price list and customer records. You will use information from these sources in some of the tasks.

Elaine Brookes, who had been private secretary to the Chairman and Managing Director for many years, left the company when it moved out of London as she did not wish to move away from her relatives and friends. She decided to set up her own business – The Brookes Office Services Agency – in which she was able to use her skills and the valuable experience gained with Systems Furniture. She leased rooms at 120 City Road, London EC1D 4LY to set up her new business.

▶ WESTSHIRE COUNTY COUNCIL

Shire Hall, Twyford, Westshire TD1 6PL

Westshire County Council, with its major offices at the Shire Hall in Twyford, is a large organi-sation and a major employer in the area. The County Council, composed of all of the elected members, is the supreme policy-making body, but the volume of business necessitates delega-tion of decision making through a framework of committees and sub-committees, each responsible for particular areas of services. Policy decisions are made by the county coun-cillors serving on the various committees, the main ones being illustrated in Fig 6.

The administration structure of the Education Department is given in Fig 7 as it is here where Paul Grant is attached for his work experience as an administrative trainee. In this capacity he assists with routine administrative duties.

▶ SAMPLE SCENARIO FOR PITMAN QUALIFICATIONS OFFICE PROCEDURES LEVEL 2 EXAMINATION

The following details are needed in the ques-tions relating to this paper.

The tasks are based at Salter Snacks Ltd, a firm manufacturing crisps, salted nuts, savoury biscuits and other snack foods.

The head office and factory are at Washington Business Park, Western Road, Exeter, Devon EX42 3HN. The firm's organisa-tional chart is given Fig 8.

The office hours are 9 am to 5.30 pm, with lunch from 12.30–1.30 pm. The offices are not currently staffed during the lunch period.

You work for Sarah Patel, Assistant Sales Manager, but in times of holidays or sickness you help out as required.

Sarah's car has a 1300 cc engine and qualifies for a mileage allowance of 32 pence per mile.

One of the organisations that you trade with is:

Orpington Social Club
48-52 Castle Street
Orpington
Kent
DA32 4KB

Telephone 01689 433566

SYSTEMS FURNITURE plc

Brookfield Industrial Estate, Twyford, Westshire TD3 2BS

Tel: 0193 384192

Telex: 342689
Fax: 0193 219673

PRICE LIST

Cat No	Description	Price (ex-warehouse) £
OFFICE FURNITURE	Systems desks – for keyboards and VDUs – with pencil drawers in sizes:	
AS1	1200mm wide 750mm deep 680mm high	300
AS2	1050mm wide 750mm deep 680mm high	280
AS3	750mm wide 750mm deep 680mm high	260
	Systems desks (split level) with pencil drawers in sizes:	
AS4	1200mm wide 750mm deep 720/680mm high	320
AS5	1050mm wide 750mm deep 720/680mm high	300
	Executive desks with pencil drawers in sizes:	
AE1	1800mm wide 850mm deep 720mm high	400
AE2	1500mm wide 850mm deep 720mm high	360
AP1	Fixed pedestal – 2 drawer	80
AP2	Fixed pedestal – 3 drawer	100
AP3	Mobile pedestal – 2 drawer	100
AP4	Mobile pedestal – 3 drawer	120

Note: All prices exclude VAT

Fig 4 Price list

SYSTEMS FURNITURE plc

Customer Records (Extract)

Name	Address	ID No	A/C Balance at 1 January 19—
Computerland plc	Avonmouth Estate 14 Southmead Road Clifton Westshire TD4 2AP	100	£200.00 Dr

Terms: Net cash 2 months after delivery – carriage paid
5% trade discount

R W Fothergill & Co	202 High Street Twyford Westshire TD1 5AT	101	

Terms: Net cash 2 months after delivery – carriage paid
10% trade discount

R L Kennedy Ltd	100 Wellington Street Fishponds Bristol BL7 9BQ	102	£50.00 Dr

Terms: Net cash one month after invoice date
Carriage paid
5% trade discount

P W Moore & Sons	Imperial House 14 Oxford Street Southampton SO3 2MG	103	

Terms: Net cash 14 days after invoice date
Carriage paid
7½% trade discount

OP Electronic Services	OP House PO Box 19 Bracknell Berks RG21 3PT	104	

Terms: Net cash within one month after delivery
Carriage paid
10% trade discount

The Square Peg Employment Agency	120 Carlton Road Twyford Westshire TD8 4RN	105	

Terms: Net cash within one month after delivery
Carriage paid
10% trade discount

Westshire County Council	Shire Hall Twyford Westshire TD1 6PL	106	

Terms: Net cash within one month after delivery
Carriage paid
5% trade discount

Fig 5 Customer records

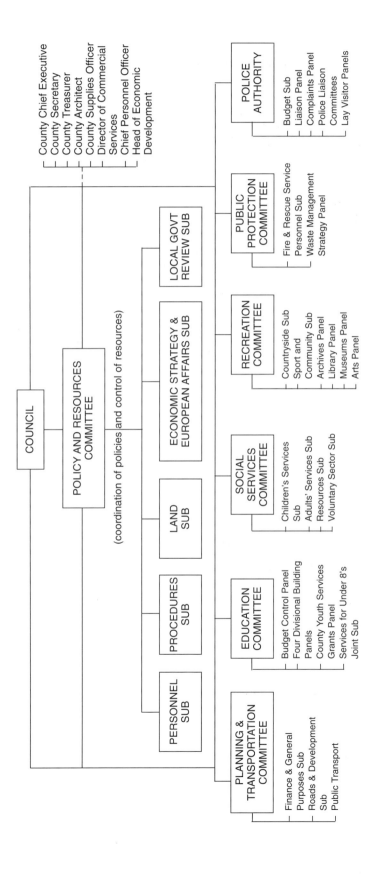

Fig 6 Council structure – principal committees and sub-committees

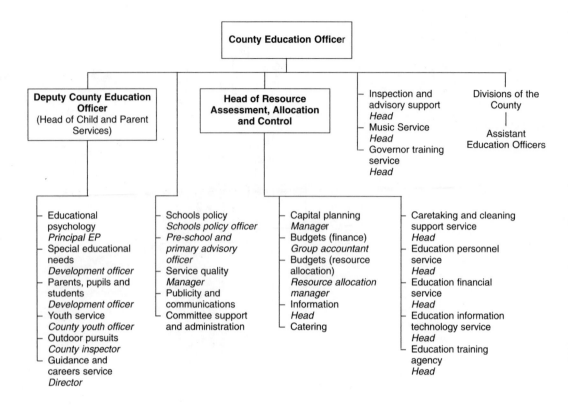

Fig 7 County Education Administration Structure Chart

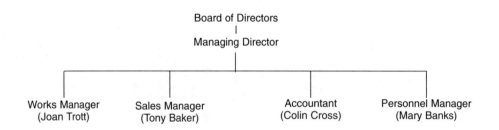

Fig 8 Organisation chart for Salter Snacks Ltd

Section A
INDUCTION

• •

Unit 1
The role and relationship of office workers in the organisation

1 Draw a chart with the headings outlined in Fig 1.1.

a Complete the entries on this chart for the organisations employing Sarah Bates, Amanda Jackson and Paul Grant showing with ticks or blocks the type of organisation and business unit in each case. Note that three entries have been made as examples.

b Cut out advertisements for office jobs from your local newspaper and complete the chart

as in a above with details of the organisations involved.

2

a Prepare an organisation chart for Systems Furniture plc containing the office staff names and positions supplied in the case study.

Organisation	Type of organisation			Business unit					
	Manufacturing/ industrial	Commercial	Services	Sole trader	Partnership	Private limited company	Public limited company	Central govt	Local govt
Examples									
Manufacturer of television sets	■						■		
Newsagent		■		■					
Department of Health			■					■	

Fig 1.1

b State which departments of this firm would deal with:
  i a complaint about faulty goods
  ii a query from a customer about a monthly statement
  iii a legal decision affecting the company
  iv the ordering of bulk stationery supplies
  v an exhibition of the firm's products to be held in Paris
  vi a suggestion from an employee concerning conditions of employment

3 Prepare an organisation chart for your school or college beginning with those who are responsible for providing the money to pay for it and ending with the students.

4 Compare the organisation chart for Compton Community Association (Fig 1) with that for the firm of solicitors (Fig 2). In what ways are they different?

5 Examine the office jobs of Sarah Bates, Amanda Jackson and Paul Grant. What office tasks and responsibilities are common to them all and what if any are their specialist roles?

6
a Which department of a large company is most likely to be responsible for:
  i maintaining a register of company shareholders

  ii ordering office equipment
  iii promoting new products
  iv establishing creditworthiness of new customers
  v reimbursing an amount equal to the value of the vouchers to restore the imprest to its original amount?
b Using the following information, draw and complete the chart in Fig 1.2 by allocating personnel under appropriate headings:

Chairman	Wages clerk
General manager	Sales representative
Buyer	Cost clerk
Board of directors	Training officer
Shop floor supervisor	Customer services
Welfare officer	manager
Factory operatives	Ledger clerk

7 Use the job advertisements given in Fig 1.3 to answer the following questions:
a Describe six main duties which the clerk in Priory Car Services would have to perform.
b Outline (i) four responsibilities of a Personnel Manager and (ii) two responsibilities of a Company Secretary.
c Describe five main duties which would be carried out in the Sales Department of Eximport plc.
d Explain three functions, related to information, which are common to the offices of each of the organisations shown in the advertisements.

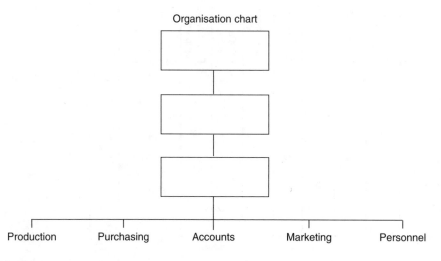

Organisation chart

| Production | Purchasing | Accounts | Marketing | Personnel |

Fig 1.2

Situations vacant

WANTED:

Clerk for general office duties in small, friendly office.

Age 18/20 – previous clerical experience preferred.

Applications to: Mrs J Grant, Priory Car Services, High Street, Meriden, Coventry.

Large manufacturing company requires a Personal Assistant for busy Company Secretary. Excellent opportunity for right applicant. Send career details to:

The Personnel Manager, Midcom Ltd
122 Kingshurst Road, Birmingham B74 5BX

We are looking for a WP Operator to join our busy workforce in the Sales Department. Some audiotyping and a good telephone manner essential.

Applications to: Mr D M Beaver, Sales Manager, Eximport plc, Stoneleigh House, Stoneleigh Road, Oldbury, B13 6BH.

Fig 1.3

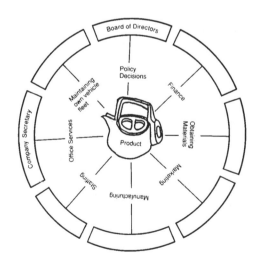

Fig 1.4

8

a The diagram in Fig 1.4 shows that the Board of Directors is responsible for policy decisions and the Company Secretary is responsible for office services. Copy the diagram and write in the empty boxes the names of the departments responsible for the functions shown.

b Name two office services which are likely to be provided centrally for the Company's Departments. For one of these services give two advantages and one disadvantage to the company of having the service provided centrally.

c Describe how the merge and sort facilities of a word processor could be used by the sales department in an advertising campaign.

9 This task is based at the firm of Underwoods Biscuits Ltd, biscuit manufacturers, which has its head office and factory in Birmingham. Its postal address is: PO Box 139, Kitts Green, Birmingham B33 2RP.

The firm is a private company owned by Arnold Underwood (Managing Director), Sarah Morrison (Company Secretary and Financial Director), Trevor Morrison (Production Director), Marcus Turnbull (Commercial Director – Buying and Marketing) and Janette Turnbull (Personnel Director). Managers, responsible to the appropriate directors, are employed in the following capacities:

Accountant
Advertising
Buying
Cashier
Chief Engineer
Export Sales
Home Sales
Office Management
Personnel
Product Development
Production
Stores
Training
Transport

a Draw up an organisation chart for Underwoods Biscuits Ltd with the information provided, using job titles only.

b For each of the managers employed by

3

JOB DESCRIPTION

Title — *Office Junior*

Department — *Administration*

Location — *Preston Road, Plymouth*

Responsible to — *George Baker – Admin Manager*

Job Summary — *General Office Duties as required by staff in department.*

Essential education — *Good general education.*

Hours of work — *9-5 Monday – Friday*

Promotion prospects — *Departmental Clerk*

Duties and responsibilities

To Be Revised

Fig 1.5

Underwoods Biscuits Ltd state a job title of one employee who would be expected to report to him/her.

(PQ OP2)

10 The Job Description (Fig 1.5) for Office Junior in the Administration Department is very out of date. Having been an Office Junior you are asked to make suggestions for the revision of the Duties and responsibilities section.

(PQ OP2)

11 This task relates to the firm of Barrington Chocolates, which has its head office and factory in Liverpool. Its postal address is: PO Box 184, Liverpool, L23 4RV.

The organisation chart in Fig 1.6 shows the board of directors and the main departments. Key areas within these departments are listed below:

Wages	Office services
Home sales	Accounts

BARRINGTON CHOCOLATES

Managing Director
(K Barrington)

BOARD OF DIRECTORS

Sale/Marketing Manager	Personnel Manager	Production Manager	Finance Manager	Purchasing Manager	Company Secretary

Fig 1.6

Advertising	Export sales
Recruitment	Works
R & D	Reception
Buying	Legal matters
Market research	Filing
Plant Engineer	Mail
Stores	Health and safety
Credit control	Training
Budgets	Insurance

Refer to the organisation chart of Barrington Chocolates shown in Fig 1.6. List the key areas under department headings.

(PQ OP2)

12 You have seen a job advertisement and are interested in applying. On enquiry you are told that an application form will not be supplied; applicants are asked to write in giving full details.

a Why does a firm require a written application?
b What type of documents would you submit as your application?
c List the sort of information that you would supply.

(PQ OP2)

13 Jane & John is a thriving, profitable organisation specialising in the manufacture and distribution of children's clothes. It is a private company, owned by Jane Sheridan and John Brewer. It employs approximately 50 people and its address is 22 Sackville Street, Bristol BS17 9ZR, telephone 0127286 3564.

At present the company is managed as follows:

John Brewer	Managing Director
Jane Sheridan	Director of Marketing
Michael Greene	Company Accountant
Robert Groves	Company Secretary
Anna Woods	Personnel Manager
William Collins	Production Manager
Peter Williams	Purchasing Manager
Eric James	Transport Manager

The above work as a management team responsible for the day-to-day running and long-term policy formulation of the company.

a Compile an organisation chart of the management team of Jane & John. Use job titles only.

b The success of the company has increased the workload of the management team and they have to introduce a system of middle management. Choose four members of the team, stating the job titles of middle managers to whom appropriate work can be delegated.

c Among the staff there are employees responsible for progress chasing, quality control and stock control. Who is their manager? Give a brief description of the main functions of their jobs.

(PQ OP2)

14 Universal Books Ltd publishes textbooks which are distributed to bookshops throughout the world. They also operate a direct sales service to schools and colleges.

The company is controlled by its owners, David Berger (Managing Director), Elizabeth Berger (Company Secretary and Financial Director) and Thomas Berger (Sales and Marketing Director).

Hannah Browning (Personnel), Michael Ellis (Production) and Joseph Delaware (Purchasing) are senior executives of the company and are members of the Board of Directors.

All members of the Board of Directors (apart from the Managing Director) have assistants/deputies who form the middle management of the organisation.

Their address is: Docklands House
Wapping Wall
London, E3 4NX
Tel: 0171-481 7369
Fax: 0171-481 6511

a Design an organisation chart of Universal Books Ltd using job titles only. Use suitable job titles for the middle management.

b Explain the purpose of having such a chart

(PQ OP2)

15 This task is based at the private company of Pinder and Moore, children's clothing manufacturers, who operate a mail order service as well as supplying various retail outlets throughout the country and a limited number of countries overseas.

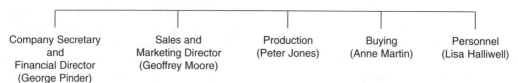

PINDER AND MOORE – ORGANISATION CHART
MANAGING DIRECTOR (Arthur Pinder)

| Company Secretary and Financial Director (George Pinder) | Sales and Marketing Director (Geoffrey Moore) | Production (Peter Jones) | Buying (Anne Martin) | Personnel (Lisa Halliwell) |

Fig 1.7

The company is owned by two brothers: Arthur Pinder (Managing Director) in overall control with the following personnel accountable to him:

George Pinder (Company Secretary and Financial Director) and a partner

Geoffrey Moore (Sales and Marketing Director)

There are three senior executives:

Peter Jones (Production)

Anne Martin (Buying)

Lisa Halliwell (Personnel)

Their address is 45 The Strand, Bristol

Tel no   Bristol 37960

Fax no   Bristol 24786

The company bankers are Central Bank PLC, 100 The Strand, Bristol.

Account No 4107689.

From the organisation chart shown in Fig 1.7 list two principal functions for each department under their respective headings.

(PQ OP2)

▶ COMPUTER/WP TASKS

16

a Use a word processor to prepare a job description for Amanda Jackson, data entry clerk in the Buying Department of Systems Furniture plc.

b Indicate (i) which items in the above job description would be standard information and would apply to the other data entry clerks at Systems Furniture plc and (ii) which items would be variable. If you were required to prepare job descriptions on your word processor for all of the data entry clerks, explain how you would do it.

▶ WORK EXPERIENCE TASKS

17 Using the firm where you are employed on work experience (part-time students use their own organisation), supply the following information for your Course Tutor:

● the nature of the organisation, ie manufacturing/industrial, commercial or services

● the business unit employed, ie sole trader, partnership, private limited company, public limited company, central government, local government, etc

● the departmental structure – draw an organisation chart showing your position in it

● the office services which are centralised

● your job description

18 Explain what you consider your employer would expect from you regarding

a your attitude to colleagues

b your relationship with customers.

19 Prepare your own cv, using a word processor.

Assess your work in working-relationship tasks against the following NVQ performance criteria

ELEMENT 4.1   Establish and maintain working relationships with other members of staff
(Level 2)

Performance criteria

a Appropriate opportunities are taken to discuss work-related matters with relevant staff.

b Essential information is passed to appropriate staff promptly and accurately.

c Effective working relationships are maintained with individuals and teams.

d Commitments to others are met within agreed time-scales.

e Methods of communication and support are suited to the needs of other staff.

Section B
OFFICE SYSTEMS, PROCEDURES AND RECORDS

• •

Unit 2
Buying and selling

1 In this assignment assume that you are employed with Paul Grant at the Westshire County Council Offices, Shire Hall, Twyford, Westshire, TD1 6PL. Using the price list issued by Systems Furniture plc (Fig 4) prepare:

a a purchases requisition on the 1st of the month

b an order form on the 2nd of the month for four split-level desks (Cat No AS5) for delivery by road to the Shire Hall, Room 201

2 In this assignment assume that you are employed by Systems Furniture plc, Twyford, Westshire.

a Prepare an invoice to Westshire County Council on the 9th of the month for the furniture ordered in 1 above. The desks were delivered on the 7th of the month by Twyford Carriers Ltd.

Terms: 5% trade discount
       Net cash within one month after delivery
       Carriage paid

b One of the desks was received with a faulty back panel and was returned. Prepare a credit note to Westshire County Council for this return on the 16th of the month.

c Prepare a statement to be sent to Westshire

County Council on the 30th of the month from the information given in *a* and *b*.

3 At the last meeting of the Sports Committee of Compton Community Association, Tony Miles, their sports secretary, was asked to make suggestions for the purchase of a table tennis table. In response to his enquiries he received quotations from four firms supplying the prices and terms in Fig 2.1.

Prepare a report for Tony Miles to make at the next meeting of the committee recommending one of these firms to supply the table tennis table and giving your reasons for this selection.

4

a Check the invoice in Fig 2.2 with the price list in Fig 4. If you discover any errors, copy out the invoice and insert the correct figures. A trade discount of 10% had been agreed.

b If you discover any errors, write a letter to Systems Furniture plc drawing their attention to them and asking them to issue an amended invoice.

5 Your employer, Mr J Edmondson, the Buyer of OP Electronic Services, has asked you to

Firm	Price £	Trade discount	VAT	Carriage	Delivery date
Mills & Moran	140	nil	not included	paid	3 months
Youth Sports	170	5%	included	fwd	2 months
Commodore	200	10%	not included	fwd	immediate
XL Sports	180	15%	included	paid	1 month

Fig 2.1

INVOICE

No 889

From :   SYSTEMS FURNITURE plc
          Brookfield Industrial Estate, Twyford, Westshire TD3 2BS

Tel: 0193 384192   Telex: 342689
                                          Fax: 0193 219673
VAT Registration No 3027560 21   Date: 1 December 19—

To: Messrs R W Fothergill & Co
      202 High Street
      Twyford
      Westshire TD1 5AT

Terms: Delivered Twyford
        Payment two months after delivery
Completion of Order No AR1289 **dated** 22 November 19--

Quantity	Description	Cat No	Price each £	Cost £	VAT rate %	VAT amount £
2	Executive desks 1800mm x 850mm x 720mm	AE1	360	720.00		
	Less trade discount 10%			72.00 792.00	$17\frac{1}{2}$	138.60
	Plus VAT			138.60 930.60		

	Delivered on: 1.12.–
	by: own van

Fig 2.2

enquire whether Systems Furniture plc manufacture a glass-fronted book case which is urgently required for the reception office. Write a letter of enquiry.

6 Systems Furniture plc have received an enquiry from The Square Peg Employment Agency for supplying six system desks 900mm wide, 750mm deep and 680mm high for wp keyboards and VDUs (not offered in their catalogue). It has been estimated that these can be supplied at the special price of £300 each, excluding VAT and a trade discount of 10% would be deducted. Delivery (free of charge) would be in one month.

Terms: net payment one month after delivery. Quotation valid for 2 months.

Prepare the quotation which Systems Furniture plc would send to The Square Peg Employment Agency in reply to this enquiry.

7

a Prepare orders to Systems Furniture plc from the following customers (refer to the customer records and price list for the relevant data). The furniture is delivered by Twyford Carriers Ltd to the customers' addresses.

Customer	Order No	Order Date	Quantity	Cat No
Computerland plc	823	10.1.19-	3	AS3
Computerland plc	831	17.1.19-	1	AS5
R L Kennedy Ltd	562	28.1.19-	1	AS2
P W Moore & Sons	3016	18.1.19-	4	AS1
P W Moore & Sons	3140	30.1.19-	2	AE2

b Prepare invoices from Systems Furniture plc to their customers on the dates given below (refer to the customer records for the relevant data):

Customer	Order No	Invoice No	Invoice Date	Delivery Date
Computerland plc	823	1234	14.1.19-	13.1.19-
Computerland plc	831	1235	22.1.19-	20.1.19-
R L Kennedy Ltd	562	1237	31.1.19-	30.1.19-
P W Moore & Sons	3016	1236	20.1.19-	20.1.19-
P W Moore & Sons	3140	1238	31.1.19-	31.1.19-

c Prepare a credit note from Systems Furniture plc to Computerland plc for one of the AS3 desks damaged in transit supplied on invoice no 1234. The credit note was dated 19 January 19– and numbered 335.

d Prepare statements as at 31 January 19– for the three customers involved in the above transactions. The following cheques had been received from these customers:

Customer	Date of Receipt	Amount £
Computerland plc	3.1.19-	200
P W Moore & Sons	28.1.19-	1000
R L Kennedy Ltd	31.1.19-	50

8

a Complete an invoice using tomorrow's date and the number V763/81 for the following goods. The customer is Evans and Grant Ltd, 177-181 Marlborough Road, Bath BA5 73G. Their order number is OE 3467. The goods will be despatched tomorrow. The terms are 5% for settlement within seven days and carriage by van is included in the price. VAT is charged at 17½%.

2 boxes of Seal Easy Wage Packets, code No 3383, at £7.50 per box

6 boxes of C6 Manilla Commercial Envelopes, code No 2073, at £5.50 per box

b Explain the purpose of:
i   a delivery note
ii   a credit note
iii a statement of account
iv a supplementary invoice

9 Use Fig 2.3 to answer questions *a* to *c*.

a Explain:
i   the purpose of each of the documents numbered 1 to 7
ii   which department in Systems Furniture plc would deal with these documents

b Select *either* the quotation *or* the despatch note and state:
i   what information should appear on the document
ii   what action would be taken on receiving the document at Systems Furniture plc

c Explain briefly how a computer might assist Systems Furniture plc to deal with the processes shown in Fig 2.3.

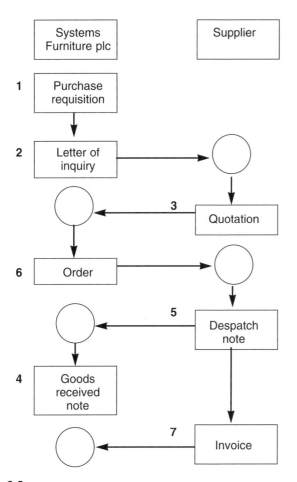

Fig 2.3

10 The Office Manager has decided to purchase new plain paper copiers – one for each department – as the old ones cannot cope with the volume of work now the business is expanding.

a Draft a letter of inquiry which can be sent to all potential suppliers, asking them to send details of their copiers and prices.

b What features would you expect a modern plain paper copier to have?

c The following quotations have been received for desktop copiers:

Name	Price	Terms	Delivery
Duplex Ltd	£350.00	20% net 1 mth	8 Wks
Carney Ltd	£390.00	15% net 1 mth	6 Wks
Parkers	£365.00	25% net 1 mth	2 Wks

Which supplier would you select? Give reasons

for your choice.

d List two other factors you would take into account before deciding on a supplier.

(*PQ OP2*)

11 In reply to the letter received from Superbuy Supermarkets plc (Fig 2.4), prepare the quotation stating the list prices and all other relevant data from the price list (Fig 2.5). Offer them a special trade discount of 10% for orders of £500 and over but point out that this quotation is only valid for two months.

(*PQ OP2*)

12 You work in the Sales Department of Caring Cosmetics, Green Acres, Nr Norwich, Norfolk, NR2 1GG. One of your regular customers is Face First of 229 O'Malley Lane, Dublin, Eire.

SUPERBUY SUPERMARKETS plc

Superbuy House, Heath Gardens, Twickenham, Middlesex TW2 3AP

Telephone: 0181 891302
Fax: 0181 892634

Our Ref: PC/FR
Your Ref:

1 April 199–

Underwoods Biscuits Ltd
PO Box 139
Kitts Green
BIRMINGHAM
B33 2RP

Dear Sirs

I shall be pleased to receive your most favourable terms
for supplying us with the following biscuits:

```
 500   200g packets of Plain Digestive Biscuits
 250   200g packets of Chocolate Digestive Biscuits
 500   500g tins of Assorted Biscuits
1000   200g packets of Cream Crackers
```

If you are able to supply these biscuits promptly to our
satisfaction and you can give us acceptable discount and
credit facilities, we would anticipate placing further
orders with you on a regular basis.

You may wish to approach our bank, Barclays Bank plc at 19
High Street, Twickenham, concerning our financial reliabil-
ity.

I look forward to receiving you quotation as soon as possible.

Yours faithfully
SUPERBUY SUPERMARKETS plc

Pauline Carrington

Pauline Carrington

Fig 2.4

They have purchased several items recently, as shown in Fig 2.6 on pages 14 and 15. They are usually given a 5% Trade Discount.

A final document is sent at the end of the month to all customers showing what they owe your company. Complete this document for Face First, using the appropriate form from Section E. Make sure everything is on the document so it is ready to be sent out.

(PQ OP1) (modified)

13 If you were working in the Marketing Department at Systems Furniture plc, how would you:

a identify the specific needs of customers when speaking to them on the telephone;

b deal with a request for advice which was outside your own responsibility;

c handle a request for confidential information by an unauthorised person;

d respond to difficult/aggressive customers who resent it when they are not able to see

```
                        199– PRICE LIST

                  UNDERWOODS BISCUITS LTD
                    Biscuit Manufacturers

            PO Box 139, Kitts Green, Birmingham B33 2RP
               Telephone: 0121 626138    Fax: 0121 642806


     Cat No                                  Weight    Price each


     SWEET BISCUITS

     50      Arrowroot                       200 g     34 p
     51      Rich Tea                        200 g     32 p
     52      Fruit Shortcake                 200 g     44 p
     53      Chocolate Cookies               200 g     48 p
     54      Fig Roll                        200 g     40 p
     55      Garibaldi                       200 g     46 p
     56      Plain Digestive                 200 g     28 p
     57      Chocolate Digestive             200 g     38 p
     58      Shortbread                      200 g     42 p
     59      Custard Cream                   200 g     32 p
     60      Bourbon                         200 g     34 p
     61      Chocolate Finger Bars           200 g     56 p
     62      Ginger Snaps                    200 g     24 p
     63.2    Assorted Biscuits (packet)      200 g     34 p
     63.5    Assorted Biscuits (tin)         500 g     75 p

     CHEESE BISCUITS

     64      Cream Crackers                  200 g     28 p
     65      Water Biscuits                  200 g     48 p
     66      Cornish Wafers                  150 g     32 p
     67.2    Assorted Cheese Biscuits (packet)  200 g  36 p
     67.5    Assorted Cheese Biscuits (tin)  500 g     78 p

     TERMS: All prices include delivery anywhere on the United Kingdom mainland
            Trade discount:  7½% on orders of £250 and over
            Cash discount:   2½% for payment within 14 days of receipt of statement
            Delivery:        By our delivery van normally within 10 days of receipt of
                             order
```

Fig 2.5

the Sales Manager on a matter which is clearly your responsibility?

14 Assume you are employed by Timepieces Ltd and are responsible for writing invoices and seeing to the distribution of various copies within the firm. You have just received the Order from County Jewellers Ltd (Fig 2.7).

Complete the invoice form (F4) using today's date.

(PQ OP1)

15 You work at Salter Snacks Ltd (*see* case study scenario).

Valley Restaurant has telephoned to complain that Invoice No E409/91 (Fig 2.8) is incorrect.

a Please check the invoice, circle any entries that are incorrect and put the correct entry alongside.

b Write a letter of apology to the company, which you will fax today, acknowledging the error and explaining how it will be rectified.

(PQ OP2)

CREDIT NOTE

No C91/7

From: Caring Cosmetics
Green Acres
Nr Norwich
Norfolk
NR2 1GG

Fax: 01603 774141

Tel: 01603 234242

Telex: KJNR 29439

VAT Registration No: 260 7534 83

Date: 8 April 199–

To: Face First
229 O'Malley Lane
DUBLIN
Eire

Ref: Invoice No 91/E/711
dated 2.4.19–

Quantity	Description	Price each £	Cost £	VAT rate %	VAT amount £
1 Box	Moisturising Cream	10	10	NIL	

INVOICE

No 91/E/711

From: Caring Cosmetics
Green Acres
Nr Norwich
Norfolk
NR2 1GG

Fax: 01603 774141

Tel: 01603 234242

Telex: KJNR 29439

VAT Registration No: 260 7534 83

Date: 2 April 199–

To: Face First
229 O'Malley Lane
DUBLIN
Eire

Completion of Order No FF83 dated 30.3.9–

Quantity	Description	Cat No	Price each £	Cost £	VAT rate %	VAT amount £
10 Boxes	Moisturising Cream	MC4	10.00	100	NIL	
50	Assorted Colour Lipsticks	L12	1.50	75	NIL	

Fig 2.6(a)

INVOICE

No 91/E/798

From: Caring Cosmetics
Green Acres
Nr Norwich
Norfolk
NR2 1GG

Fax: 01603 774141

Tel: 01603 234242

Telex: KJNR 29439

VAT Registration No: 260 7534 83

Date: 10 April 199–

To: Face First
229 O'Malley Lane
DUBLIN
Eire

Completion of Order No FF98   dated 12.4.19–

Quantity	Description	Cat No	Price each £	Cost £	VAT rate %	VAT amount £
20 Bottles	Handcream	N12	1.20	24.00	NIL	

INVOICE

No 91/E/740

From: Caring Cosmetics
Green Acres
Nr Norwich
Norfolk
NR2 1GG

Fax: 01603 774141

Tel: 01603 234242

Telex: KJNR 29439

VAT Registration No: 260 7534 83

Date: 10 April 199–

To: Face First
229 O'Malley Lane
DUBLIN
Eire

Completion of Order No FF90   dated 2.4.19–

Quantity	Description	Cat No	Price each £	Cost £	VAT rate %	VAT amount £
4 Cartons	Shampoo	S41	50	200	NIL	
10 Cards	Nail Scissors	K20	4	40	NIL	
10 Cards	Combs	S3	1	10	NIL	

Fig 2.6(b) (Note: VAT is a sales tax)

County Jewellers Ltd
100 High Street, Newton N14 4RD

ORDER NO: 331

Tel: 3792 248921
Fax: 3792 448921

DATE: (Yesterday's date)

Timepieces Ltd
Century Works
Bridgeway
19 6HY

Please supply:

Cat No	Quantity	Description	Price each £
6-A70	8	Ladies Fun Watch – enamelled case	30.00
6-A75	4	Ladies Fashion Watch – gold plate case with black roman numerals	40.00
6-A82	4	Ladies Quality Watch – gold plated case – jewelled movement	100.00

DELIVERY: Immediate

Signed   *A B Somerton*
For County Jewellers Ltd

Fig 2.7

16

a i Using the Pinder & Moore mail order price list for children's clothes (*see* Fig 2.9) respond to the letter from Mrs Leaf (Fig 2.10) by completing the invoice.

ii Calculate the total.

iii Work out her discount of 12.5% if she pays the full amount before the end of the month. Total her bill.

b Explain the difference between a 'cash discount' and a 'trade discount'.

(PQ OP2)

▶ COMPUTER/WP TASKS

17

a Use a word processor to prepare standard forms for letters of enquiry and quotations. Enter the details required in Tasks 5 and 6 and print out one copy of each.

b Use a computer accounting package to set up the customer records of Systems Furniture plc (Fig 5) and key in the transactions given in Task 7 to provide printouts for the invoices, credit notes and statements.

▶ WORK EXPERIENCE TASKS

18 Work in the buying department:
● prepare letters of enquiry for supplying goods
● request quotations from suppliers
● complete order forms

Work in the accounts department:

● check incoming invoices for certification and payment
● prepare statements

Work in the sales department:

● prepare quotations
● prepare invoices and credit notes
● deal with customer complaints and queries

INVOICE   No E409/91

SALTER SNACKS LTD
Washington Business Park
Western Road
Exeter
Devon
EX42 3HN

Telephone: 01392 223322
Fax: 01392 111222

To Valley Restaurant
    The Square
    Reigate
    Surrey RH42 1PQ   Date xx xxxxxxx 199x

Quantity	Description	Cat No	Unit Price £	Cost £
90 pkts	Salted peanuts	K122	0.22	198.00
60 pkts	Cashew nuts	K133	0.32	19.20
12 boxes	Salt & Vinegar crisps	P134	2.50	30.00
10 Jars	Stuffed olives	S101	1.40	14.00
				333.20
				24.99
				309.21

Less 7.5% trade discount

Fig 2.8

BACK TO SCHOOL
PRICE LIST
BOYS

	Catalogue No	Sizes	Price
Shirts (long sleeves)	27114	43/46 ins	7.99 pack of two
		48/51, 53/55	8.99 pack of two
Shirt (long sleeves)	27115	43/46, 48/51	6.99 each
Trousers (polyester)	28444	23/24	7.99
		25/26/27/28	8.99
		29/30	11.99
V-Neck Jumpers (plain knit)	28449	43/46	4.99
		53/55	5.99
		58/60	7.99
V-neck Cable Sweater	29771	43/46	11.99
		48/51, 53/55	12.99
		58/60, 62/64	15.99
GIRLS			
Skirts (straight)	34444	48, 51, 53	8.99
		55, 58, 60	11.99
Skirts (pleated)	34721	48, 51, 53	7.99
		55, 58, 60	9.99
Blouses (long sleeves)	36671	39/41, 43/46	7.99 pack of two
		48/51, 53/55	8.99 " " "
Blouses (long sleeves)	36672	39/41, 43/46	6.99
		48/51, 53/55	7.99
Cardigan long-line	34660	39/41, 43/46	10.99
		48/51, 53/55	11.99
		62/64, 67/69	14.99

Colours: Red, Royal Blue, Navy, Bottle Green, Grey
Shirts and Blouses are available in White, Pale Blue and Light Grey only

Measurements: Order by height only except for boys' trousers which are in waist
measurements. See back of your catalogue for full details of sizing.

Fig 2.9

Agents No: 0171-345769

49 Fare Street
Midsomer Norton
Avon
BA2 4GT

Pinder & Moore
45 The Strand
Bristol

Dear Sirs

I would like to order the following children's clothes from your 'Back to School' leaflet for my customers.

BOYS:- 3 pairs of trousers cat no. 28444 sizes 23/24 ⎱ Grey
 1 pair " " " " " sizes 29/30 ⎰ Grey
 Pack of 2 shirts cat no. 27114 size 53/55 - pale blue
 1 V-neck jumper " " 28449 " 53/55 - Navy
 " " " " " " " 58/60 - Navy

GIRLS:- 1 pleated skirt cat no. 34721 size 53 - Grey
 1 straight " " " 34444 " 48 - Grey
 1 " " " " " " 60 - Grey
 3 packs of 2 blouses cat no. 36671 size 41 - White
 1 long-line cardigan " " 34660 " 41 - Navy

Would you please also send me some order forms for future use as I have run out.
 Yours faithfully
 R Leaf (Mrs)

Fig 2.10

Assess your work in these tasks against the following NVQ performance criteria

ELEMENT 7.2   Prepare a variety of documents
(Level 2)

Performance criteria
a Instructions are understood.
b Completed documentation meets the requirements of the workplace.
c Layout, spelling, grammar and punctuation are consistent and in accordance with conventions and house style.
d Corrections, when appropriate, are unobtrusive.
e Security and confidentiality of information is maintained.
f Copies and originals are correctly collated and routed, as directed.

g Where work is not achievable within specified deadlines reasons are promptly and accurately reported.
h Work is achieved within agreed deadlines.

ELEMENT 10.1   Order goods and services
(Level 2)

Performance criteria
a Instructions are understood before ordering goods and services.
b Ordering of goods and services is in accordance with authorised procedures.
c Documentation for ordering goods is completed in accordance with specified procedures.
d Competitive prices have been obtained prior to placing order, where applicable.

Unit 3
Stock control

In assignments **1** to **3** assume that you are employed with Sarah Bates at the solicitors R W Fothergill & Co.

1 Sarah advises you that one of the items of stationery on the stock list (Fig 3) needs to be re-ordered from the stationery suppliers - Law Stationers plc, 182 Duncan Terrace, London N1 5BX.

a Select the item which you consider needs to be re-ordered and complete an order form for an appropriate quantity. Find out and use the current price for this item.

b Prepare a stock control card for the item ordered in *a* and enter on it the balance at 1 January and details of the order.

c The goods are received a week later with invoice No T462. Record this on the stock control card.

2

a Complete a stock requisition on the 3rd of the month for 100 postcards (two packets).

b Prepare a stock control card for this item and enter the balance on 1 January and the requisition in *a*.

3

a Prepare stock control cards for stock items 104, 106 and 114 and enter the opening balances.

b Enter the stock requisitions (Fig 3.1) on the stock control cards.

c If you consider that any of the items require restocking, prepare an order for an appropriate quantity to Law Stationers plc as referred to in 1. Find out and use the current price for this item. If an order is prepared, enter it on the stock control card.

STOCK REQUISITION			
No _1_			
Date _2 January 19-_			
Quantity	Description	Stock Ref No	Staff/dept
4 reams	A5 plain bond paper	104	} G Street
3 reams	A4 bank paper	106	
Signed _G Street_		Storekeeper's initials	
Authorised _P. Sherwin_			

STOCK REQUISITION			
No _2_			
Date _3 January 19-_			
Quantity	Description	Stock Ref No	Staff/dept
5 reams	A5 plain bond paper	104	} L Tyler
5 reams	A4 bank paper	106	
Signed _L Tyler_		Storekeeper's initials	
Authorised _P. Sherwin_			

STOCK REQUISITION			
No _3_			
Date _4 January 19-_			
Quantity	Description	Stock Ref No	Staff/dept
6 reams	A4 bank paper	106	} P Whitehead
4 packets (25 in each)	C5 envelopes	114	
Signed _P Whitehead_		Storekeeper's initials	
Authorised _P. Sherwin_			

Fig 3.1

4

a Complete a stock control card with the following information:

Description: Staples No 900 6mm (Box 500)
Supplier: George Betts Ltd,
          Paradise Street, Hertford
Max: 100 boxes *Min:* 30 boxes
In stock on 8 February: 55 boxes

9.2 issued 5 boxes to sales, reqn No 210
10.2 issued 3 boxes to works, reqn No 132
14.2 issued 10 boxes to typing pool, reqn No 310
16.2 received 60 boxes from George Betts Ltd, invoice No 8745
17.2 issued 5 boxes to purchasing, reqn No 78
20.2 issued 4 boxes to planning, reqn No 402

b Why was it desirable that the 60 boxes of staples from George Betts Ltd should be received by 16 February?

5 The stock card in Fig 3.2 has been incorrectly completed and you discover there are only 15 reams of headed bond paper in stock.

a Complete another stock card to show the correct position.

b How do the headings 'Max' and 'Min' on stock record cards help to ensure an adequate supply of stock?

6 The Office Manager is concerned about the wastage of stationery in the office. Headed A4 paper is stockpiled in desk drawers, mixed up with loose copy paper and half-used bottles of correcting fluid. Half-empty packets of bank and bond paper are lying open on tops of filing cabinets, collecting dirt. Every evening the waste paper baskets are filled with discarded headed paper. The office junior is frequently being sent to purchase ball point pens using petty cash. Work is frequently held up as particular items of stationery run out.

a i Write a memo to all office staff informing them that you have been made responsible for stationery control. Use your own name and today's date.

ii Outline a system of stock control which uses a lockable store room, stock cards and requisition forms. Explain the rea-

STOCK RECORD				
Ref: GB/2651			Item: Bond A4 grey headed	
Max: 100 reams		Min: 20 reams	Reorder: 40 reams	
Date	Ref	In	Out	Balance
20.5				20
21.5	Invoice 67924A	80		80
25.5	Req No 32	10		90
27.5	Req No 41		20	70
1.6	Req No 50		20	90
3.6	Req No 63		15	75
18.6	Req No 84		20	55

Fig 3.2

sons for these controls.

iii Include three rules to be followed at each work station to reduce stationery waste.

b On checking the stationery stock card in Fig 3.3 the supervisor found several errors which she has indicated. Please enter the correct details on a stock record card for:

A4 Bank White

Max: 10 reams

Min: 2 reams

Re-order: 4 reams

Ref: Ban12

Check and enter the correct balance.

7

a From the stock requisitions in Fig 3.4 select those relating to A4 bond paper white 74 gsm (ref A4HW) and record the items in date order on a stock control card. Twenty-three

reams were in stock before the entries were made.

b Make out a purchase requisition to the Purchasing Department ordering a suitable quantity of A4 bond paper white 74 gsm to make up the stock (maximum stock figure is set at 50). This paper is normally supplied in multiples of 10 reams. Sign the requisition and date it with today's date; the requisition reference is ST493.

8 You have been asked to be responsible for the issuing of stationery.

Please write a memo to the Manager letting him know the following:

a What type of storage facilities should be provided.

b The rules you would like to draw up for the issuing of stock.

(PQ OP1)

STATIONERY STOCK CARD				
Ref: BON 12			Item: A4 Bank White	
Max: 2 reams		Min: 10 reams	Reorder: 4 reams	
Date	Ref	In	Out	Balance
10.5.–	Invoice 374	8		8
11.5.–	Sales		2	10
12.5.–	Accounts		1	11
	Please correct			

Fig 3.3

STOCK REQUISITION		
To: Stores No: S 46		
From: Marketing Date: 22 June 19–		
Quantity	Ref	Description
4 Reams	A4 BW	A4 Bank Paper White
4 Reams	A4 LW	A4 Bond Paper White 61 gsm
Authorization: A M Mitchell		

STOCK REQUISITION		
To: Stores No: AD 72		
From: Advertising Date: 21 June 19–		
Quantity	Ref	Description
3 Reams	A4 LW	A4 Bond Paper White 61 gsm
2 Reams	A4 CH	A4 Bond Paper White 74 gsm (headed)
Authorization: B S Brophy		

STOCK REQUISITION		
To: Stores No: W 15		
From: Wages Date: 22 June 19–		
Quantity	Ref	Description
2 Reams	A4 HW	A4 Bond Paper White 74 gsm
1 Ream	A4 BW	A4 Bank Paper White
Authorization: A T Thomas		

STOCK REQUISITION		
To: Stores No: P 163		
From: Purchasing Date: 23 June 19–		
Quantity	Ref	Description
5 Reams	A4 LW	A4 Bond Paper White 61 gsm
3 Reams	A4 HW	A4 Bond Paper White 74 gsm
Authorization: P Wilder		

STOCK REQUISITION		
To: Stores No: P 164		
From: Purchasing Date: 24 June 19–		
Quantity	Ref	Description
3 Reams	A4 CH	A4 Bond Paper White 74 gsm (headed)
Authorization: P Wilder		

STOCK REQUISITION		
To: Stores No: AD 73		
From: Advertising Date: 23 June 19–		
Quantity	Ref	Description
6 Reams	A4 HW	Bond Paper A4 White 74 gsm
Authorization: B S Brophy		

STOCK REQUISITION		
To: Stores No: A 11		
From: Accounts Date: 24 June 19–		
Quantity	Ref	Description
2 Reams	A4 HW	A4 White Bond Paper 74 gsm
Authorization: D Cooper		

STOCK REQUISITION		
To: Stores No: S 45		
From: Marketing Date: 20 June 19–		
Quantity	Ref	Description
4 Reams	A4 HW	Bond Paper A4 White 74 gsm
Authorization: A M Mitchell		

Fig 3.4

EXTRACT FROM BUSINESS AND SECRETARIAL BOOKS CATALOGUE

FINANCIAL ACCOUNTING	1991	UK	356pp	0 09 756321 1	£12.50
STATISTICS FOR BUSINESS	1989	UK	249pp	0 07 816502 5	£10.00
FILING	1988	UK	125pp	0 08 436217 6	£4.99
BUSINESS STUDIES IN THE 1990s	1991	UK	216pp	0 09 909214 3	£6.50
COMPOSING AT THE TYPEWRITER	1992	UK	150pp	0 08 385761 6	£3.99
THE SECRETARY AT WORK	1991	UK	304pp	0 09 907316 2	£11.75
TYPEWRITING, BK 1	1992	UK	186pp	0 09 142877 4	£7.00
TYPEWRITING, BK 2	1992	UK	205pp	0 09 142965 4	£7.50
KEYBOARDING ON COMPUTERS	1993	UK	158pp	0 09 137215 4	£5.99
TYPEWRITING ASSIGNMENTS	1993	UK	308pp	0 09 138456 4	£10.25
COMPUTING FOR STUDENTS	1992	UK	133pp	0 09 073421 4	£4.50
INTRO TO WORD PROCESSING	1992	UK	200pp	0 09 064892 4	£6.50
WORD PROCESSING BK 5	1993	UK	280pp	0 09 065214 4	£8.00
AUDIO TYPING MADE EASY	1989	UK	90pp	0 08 997554 6	£4.50

TERMS

Instructors may request an inspection copy of any book suitable for group or class use.

Discounts will be given for books ordered directly by schools and colleges.

All prices may be changed without notice.

Fig 3.5

9 At present Pinder & Moore's stock control system is still done by a stock control clerk hand writing control cards, and although the stock control is centralised it takes time to keep up with stock movements and consequently items are frequently unavailable especially at the beginning of the new school year.

a Write a short report explaining ways of updating their stock control systems using new technology.

b In the report mention how the various agents and branches could be involved.

c Explain the terms 'maximum' and 'minimum' stock levels.

(*PQ OP2*)

10

a Using the extract from Universal Books' Business and Secretarial Books Catalogue (Fig 3.5), prepare the invoice (F5) for the books requested by Mrs Palmer of Hillside School (Fig 3.6). Allow a direct sales discount of 12.5%. There is no sales tax. The order will be delivered by van tomorrow.

b Update the Stock Control Cards (F9) for each book.

(*PQ OP2*)

▶ **COMPUTER/WP TASKS**

11

a Use a computer stock control package to answer Task 3. Figure 3 provides the information required for opening the data file.

b Visit a local store which uses the bar coding system at the cash tills and collect a package containing a bar code and the receipt which was produced for you from scanning the bar code (as illustrated in Fig 3.3 of *Office Procedures*).

> Hillside School
> Woodlands Road
> SIDCUP
> Kent DA16 3JP
> (Yesterday's date)

Dear Sirs

I would like to order the following books from your Business and Secretarial Books catalogue:

0 09 909214 3 "Business Studies in the 1990s"

20 copies

0 09 907316 2 "The Secretary at work"

15 copies

Please let me have these as soon as possible. The invoice should be addressed to me at the above address and should include any discounts applicable.

Yours faithfully,

H Palmer

H. PALMER (Mrs)
Head of Department of
Business Studies

Fig 3.6

► **WORK EXPERIENCE TASKS**

12 Work in the stores:

- check receipts of stock against copy orders
- enter receipts and withdrawals of stock on stock records
- assist with stock-taking checks
- file stock records

Assess your work in these tasks against the following NVQ performance criteria

ELEMENT 9.1   Order, monitor and maintain stock
(Level 2)

Performance criteria
a Sufficient stocks are maintained to meet current and anticipated demands.
b Ordering of stock is in accordance with organisational procedures.
c Stock is handled and securely stored in conformity with organisational requirements.
d Stock check and inventory reconciliation are as instructed and any discrepancies promptly reported to the appropriate person.
e Incoming deliveries are checked against order and any discrepancies promptly reported to the appropriate person.
f Records are up to date, legible and accurate.

ELEMENT 9.2   Issue stock items on request
(Level 2)

Performance criteria
a Issue of stock is in accordance with organisational procedures.
b Requests are responded to promptly and accurately.
c Stock is handled and securely stored in compliance with organisational requirements.
d Records are up to date, legible and accurate.
e Damage to stock is promptly and accurately reported to the appropriate person.

Unit 4
Receipts and payments

1 Leslie Calder, treasurer of Compton Community Association, has opened a bank current account for the Association and pays most of his bills by cheque. This week he has to pay £25 to Granada Films plc for the hire of a film.

a Complete a cheque for Leslie to send to Granada Films plc.

b At the next management committee Leslie will be expected to present a short report on a suggestion that the club should use the direct debit system for paying the regularly occurring bills. Prepare this report explaining the advantages and disadvantages of taking this course of action and suggesting which of the bills could be paid by this method.

2 In this assignment assume that you are employed by R W Fothergill & Co to assist Luke McCabe, the accounts clerk. They have an account with Midland Bank plc (account No 20132649).

a This morning's post contains the following remittances:

Remitter	Method of payment	Amount £	
J Spelling & Co	Cheque	17.42	
Callaghan Bros	Cash	7.50	(1 £5 note, 2 £1 coins and a 50p coin)
Systems Furniture plc	Cheque	150.00	
Westshire County Council	Cheque	29.40	
R Morgan	PO	3.50	
B Harris	Cash	22.48	(4 £5 notes, 2 £1 coins, 45p in silver and 3p in bronze coins)

Prepare a paying-in slip to pay these remittances into the bank today.

b Prepare a cheque in payment of the amended invoice for assignment 4 of Unit 2 (p 8).

3 In this assignment you are assisting Paul Prince, wages clerk with Systems Furniture plc.

a Complete the necessary bank documents to arrange for the following employees to receive their wages by credit transfer:

Employee	Account No	Amount £	Bank	Bank code No
K Ash	04923412	146.75	Midland, Twyford	40-61-22
N Tilling	12365489	78.00	Lloyds, Salisbury	30-42-39
P Patel	44823612	100.43	Barclays, Andover	20-63-41
C Vaughan	31324896	94.20	Lloyds, Twyford	30-42-32

b The firm agrees to a Social Club Committee's suggestion that an annual subscription should be paid to the Royal Cancer Research Fund. Complete the appropriate bank form to arrange for a standing order of £100 to be paid annually from the firm's current account starting on 1 January next year for a period of five years as a donation to the Royal Cancer Research Fund. It is to be paid into account No 20124896 of the Barclays Bank plc, York branch, code No 20-42-31. Quote the reference No AP14632. The firm has not previously subscribed to this fund.

4 When preparing the bank paying-in slip on 1 March 19– Naomi Tilling put the cheques in Fig 4.1 on one side as she did not think the bank would accept them in their present form.

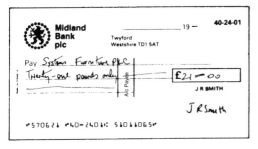
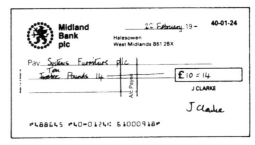

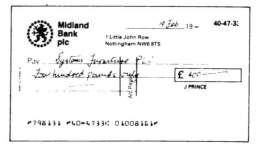

Fig 4.1

Why do you think they were unacceptable? What action do you suggest that Naomi should take with these four cheques?

5 Mr L A Scott, the home sales manager of Systems Furniture plc, has made arrangements to visit a customer in London tomorrow and he has asked you to cash a cheque for £50 at the firm's bank.

a Complete a cheque to provide the necessary cash.

b If Mr Scott finds that he has not drawn out sufficient for his purposes what methods could he use to obtain additional cash while he is in London?

6 Mr W Warboys of Cenotaph House, East Parton, Lincs received his bank statement today and an extract is printed in Fig 4.2. Make a list of the dates on which transactions are recorded and opposite each date write a full explanation of the entry.

Mr W Warboys
Cenotaph House
East Parton
Lincs

In account with
British Bank Limited
East Parton Branch

Account No   00761571

Date	Detail	Debit	Credit	Balance
19–				
13 Feb	Balance forward			90.02
15 Feb	Automobile Assn DD	16.50		
	Fleet Yacht Club SO	40.00		33.52
17 Feb	046614	38.27		4.75 OD
20 Feb	046616	15.32		20.07 OD
21 Feb	From D/A		100.00	
	G B Tankers CT		248.46	328.39
24 Feb	Charges	6.50		321.89
	046615	123.14		198.75

Fig 4.2

7 You are working in the General Office of a small firm called Easiglide Ltd.

a This morning you opened the mail and among the correspondence were the following payments:

   i   cheque for £75.32 sent by Dickenson & Brown

   ii crossed postal order for £6.50 from Miss L Waters

   iii registered packet from Joe Twining containing:

       1 × £10 note

       3 × £5 notes

       2 × £1 coins

Enter these in a remittances book.

b During the lunch hour you were looking after the Reception Desk and Mrs L M Oldenbourg from Central Cleaners called with a £16 cash refund (3 × £5 notes, 2 × 50p coins) on a cleaning bill for office curtains. Make out a receipt for Mrs Oldenbourg.

c You are asked to take the payments received in the morning mail to the bank, together with the amount from Central Cleaners. Complete the paying-in book to cover the total. Your company's account number is 50347479.

d Explain why Joe Twining sent his payment in a registered packet.

e Give the reason why Miss Walters crossed the £6.50 postal order.

f Explain in detail why a written record is kept of cash receipts and payments.

8 Irene Digwell, PO Box 100, Spalding, Lincs. PE8 2RA, is in the nursery business selling fruit trees, shrubs and spring bulbs by mail order and at garden centres. Many of her customers pay in cash, for which she issues receipts and retains carbon copies for her own records.

a For what purposes will Irene Digwell use the carbon copies of receipts issued?

b Why do you think her customers will require receipts for their cash payments?

c If customers pay by cheque should they ask for a receipt?

d Irene Digwell receives an order accompanied by cash for six Victoria Plum Trees @ £12.95 from Mr R H Lane, 2 The Precinct, Eccles, Manchester, M21 6PR in this morning's post. Mr Lane had deducted 2½% cash discount

for an order in excess of £50 which was allowable. Prepare the receipt you would issue to Mr Lane acknowledging receipt of his cash payment.

9

a Check the two expenses claim forms in Fig 4.3 for accuracy, referring to the mileage chart in Fig 4.4. Both employees travel from Twyford. A margin of error in mileage up to 10% may be given to allow for diversions, etc. The current mileage allowance is 18p per mile. Say, with reasons, if you would pass the forms for payment.

b Complete an expenses claim form for Mr L A Scott, the Home Sales Manager of Systems Furniture plc, who works at the Head Office in Twyford. His personal details are as follows:

Employee No: 106

Departmental Code: 05

Bank code: 401839

Bank account no: 20583493

3/4 February:	Return car journey to London
	Stayed at the Piccadilly Hotel – £94.00
	(including £14 VAT)
	Meals: £47.00
	(including £7 VAT)
	Parking fees: £5
10/11 February:	Return car journey to Sheffield
	Stayed at Royal Victoria Hotel – £58.75
	(including £8.75 VAT)
	Meals: £44.65
	(including £6.65 VAT)
20 February:	Return car journey to Plymouth
	Meals: £28.20
	(including £4.20 VAT)
	Parking fee: £1
27 February:	Return train journey to Exeter: £8
	Meals: £15.28
	(including £2.28 VAT)

10 Complete an expenses claim form for a course you attended at the Salisbury College of

EMPLOYEE EXPENSES CLAIM

Name: R. N. Young   Employee No. | 0 | 1 | 8 | 2 | Departmental Code: | 1 | 1 |

Bank Code: | 2 | 0 | 1 | 9 | 3 | 6 | Bank account No. | 1 | 2 | 4 | 5 | 3 | 8 | 9 | 1 |

Date 19–	Particulars	Car Mileage	Public Transport	Car Hire	Hotel accom- modation	Meals		Sundries		Total		VAT Recover- able	
4 Feb	Visit to London office	380				23	00	5	00	28	00		
	(Parking £5)												
25 "	Meeting at Southampton	180				13	80			13	80		
	with P. W. Moore												
27 "	Motor Vehicle	100				11	50	2	00	11	50		
	Exhibition at Bristol												
	(Parking £2)												
	Total Mileage	660						Mileage Amount		118	80		
								TOTAL AMOUNT DUE		172	10		

These expenses have been wholly, exclusively and necessarily incurred on authorised business

Signed *R N Young*

Authorised   Date   1 March 19–

EMPLOYEE EXPENSES CLAIM

Name: N. T. Benney   Employee No. | 0 | 1 | 0 | 1 | Departmental Code: | 0 | 4 |

Bank Code: | 4 | 0 | 1 | 3 | 6 | 9 | Bank account No. | 2 | 8 | 7 | 6 | 4 | 3 | 5 | 1 |

Date 19–	Particulars	Car Mileage	Public Transport	Car Hire	Hotel accom- modation	Meals		Sundries		Total		VAT Recover- able	
5 Feb	IPM Conference at	195				14	10			14	10	2	10
	Hereford (Parking £5)												
19/20 "	Visiting agent in L'pool	440			58	75	28	20	2	00	88	95	12	95
	(Pking £2) Hotel St George												
26 "	Training Exhibition at	180				16	45			16	45	2	45
	Cardiff												
	Visiting sick employee in Twyford	8											
	Total Mileage	823						Mileage Amount		148	14		
								TOTAL AMOUNT DUE		267	64	17	50

These expenses have been wholly, exclusively and necessarily incurred on authorised business

Signed *N T Benney*

Authorised *P Green*   Date   2 March 19–

Fig 4.3

BIRMINGHAM

85	BRISTOL											
107	45	CARDIFF										
157	81	120	EXETER									
55	53	58	126	HEREFORD								
98	178	200	250	116	LIVERPOOL							
63	74	109	152	80	165	OXFORD						
199	125	164	45	168	294	193	PLYMOUTH					
112	52	98	91	102	217	62	134	SALISBURY				
87	179	202	249	148	76	143	293	205	SHEFFIELD			
128	75	122	108	128	237	65	149	23	205	SOUTHAMPTON		
126	48	87	32	95	220	121	75	67	221	89	TWYFORD	
117	119	155	170	135	210	56	215	82	167	78	167	LONDON

Fig 4.4 Mileage chart

Technology. The course fee had been paid in advance. You were permitted to use your motorcycle and were able to claim 10p per mile from your home in Twyford. You paid £3 for your lunch.

11 Interviews were held yesterday for the position of Export Manager. Prior to passing the Expenses Claims for authorisation, check and complete the form for Paul Franks from Liverpool (Fig 4.5), who has partially filled his in, making any necessary corrections, and make one out for Charles Frazer from Bristol. Both candidates stayed at the same hotel and were allowed £14.50 towards their evening meal. Use the mileage chart (Fig 4.4) to check distances and note that mileage is payable at 35p per mile.

(PQ OP2)

12

a Complete a cheque on 5 April 19– for signature by the Cashier to settle Midland Flour Milling Company's account for March (Fig 4.6).

b Is it necessary to request a receipt for this payment? Explain the reason for your answer.

c Check the invoice received from the Midland Flour Milling Co (Fig 4.7) with the order (Fig 4.8). If you find any errors write a memo to the Accountant explaining the reasons for them and stating the correct figures for the invoice. A trade discount of 7½% had been agreed.

(PQ OP2)

13 Check the expense claim (Fig 4.9) which has been received from Mr J Powdrill by referring to the mileage chart. Write a memo to J Powdrill advising him of any discrepancies you find. The Company pays 30p per mile.

(PQ OP2)

14 Use the scenario on page xvi for this task.

Sarah Patel has handed you a page from her diary (Fig 4.10) showing her expenses for the week commencing Monday 29th. Work out her car mileage from the chart in Fig 4.4 and complete the expense claim form (F28).

(PQ OP2)

CLAIM FOR EXPENSES

Claimant's Name: _____ Department _____

Date	Particulars of travel	Car £	Rail/ Air* £	Hotel Accom* £	Meals* £	Others*† eg taxis £	Daily Totals £
	By car from Liverpool to attend Interview for post of Export Manager						
	Total mileage 570 miles @ 30p per mile	171.00		85.00	14.50		
	*Bills and receipts should be attached †Please specify other expenses overleaf			Grand total		£	
	Checked by _____	Authorised by _____ Date _____					

Fig 4.5

STATEMENT

From: MIDLAND FLOUR MILLING CO
       136 Derby Road, Bramcote, Nottingham, NG8 4LT

Telephone: 01602 314322   Fax: 01602 483196

To:
Underwoods Biscuits Ltd
PO Box 139
Birmingham B33 2RP

Date: 31 March 199–

Terms: 2½% cash discount for payment within 14 days of the receipt of statement; otherwise net cash within one month

Date	Details	Ref No	Dr £	Cr £	Balance £
199– March 1	Balance	b/f			119.00 DR
8	Invoice	S193	146.00		265.00
12	Payment	C120		119.00	146.00
18	Invoice	S207	843.50		989.50
22	Returns	R63		126.75	862.75

The last amount in the balance column is the amount owing

Fig 4.6

INVOICE

No S333

MIDLAND FLOUR MILLING CO
136 Derby Road, Bramcote, Nottingham NG8 4LT

Tel: 01602 314322

Fax: 01602 483196
Date: 14 April 199–

To:
```
Underwoods Biscuits Ltd
PO Box 139
Kitts Green
Birmingham B33 2RP
```

Terms: 2½% cash discount for payment within 14 days of the receipt
of statement; otherwise net cash within one month
Completion of Order No AB1096 dated 7 April 199–

Quantity	Description	Cat No	Price each £	Cost £
80	50 kg bags of plain white flour	R196	12.60	1 008.00
50	50 kg bags of wholemeal flour	R162	13.20	680.00 1 688.00
	Less 7½% trade discount			126.60 1 814.60

Fig 4.7

ORDER

No AB 1096

UNDERWOODS BISCUITS LTD
PO Box 139 Kitts Green, Birmingham B33 2RP

Tel: 01800 626138

Fax: 01800 642806
Date: 7 April 199–

To:
```
Midland Flour Milling Co
136 Derby Road
Bramcote
Nottingham NG8 4LT
```

Please supply:

Quantity	Description	Your Cat No	Price each £
80	50 kg bags of plain white flour	R196	12.60
50	50 kg bags of wholemeal flour	R162	13.20
	Carriage paid/~~forward~~		
	Deliver by: Road/~~rail~~ promptly to: the above address	*J Snow* Buyer	

Fig 4.8

Date	Particulars	Car Mileage	Public Transport	Car hire	Hotel Accommodation	Meals	Sundries	Total	VAT Recoverable
23/5	Return trip to Bristol from Liverpool	356	–	– –	72 00	21 00	– –	93 00	
28/5	Liverpool Sheffield Return	175	–	– –	· –	23 00	– –	23 00	
							Mileage Amount	159 30	
	Total Mileage	531							
							Total amount due	275 30	

Name: J. Powdrill **Employee No** 3 4 0 6 **Departmental Code** S A
Bank code 2 0 1 7 2 5 **Bank account No** 2 0 1 6 7 3 6 2

These expenses have been wholly, exclusively and necessarily incurred on authorised business

Signed *J Powdrill*

Authorised   Date

Fig 4.9

▶ COMPUTER/WP TASKS

15

a Use a word processor to prepare a receipt form for your firm, Supersales plc, and then enter the following details of cash receipts (received today) to provide fully completed receipt forms:

Remitter	Sale Details	Amount £
J L Clarkson	Single duvet covers	10.95
R O Mann	Cloverleaf tablemats	7.75
P Sperring	Brabantia ironing board	15.95
T Watson	Shilton handbag	14.99

b Using the data file prepared for Task 17 (Unit 2) enter the following transactions for February:

Cheques received

		£
3 February	P W Moore & Sons	276.50
10 February	P W Moore & Sons	765.90
14 February	Computerland plc	568.10
21 February	R L Kennedy Ltd	305.90

Invoices sent

			Goods	VAT
		Inv no.	£	£
5 February	Computerland plc	1280	570.00	99.75
18 February	R L Kennedy Ltd	1301	95.00	16.63
23 February	P W Moore & Sons	1328	222.00	38.85

Print out statements at 28 February 19–.

▶ WORK EXPERIENCE TASKS

16 Work in the cashier's section:
Receipts:

- check cash received and, if necessary, give change
- complete receipt forms for cash received
- maintain daily totals of cash received
- scrutinise and record cheques received
- complete vouchers for payment by credit card after checking cards and signatures for validity
- pay cash and cheques into the bank, completing paying-in slips
- withdraw cash from the bank

Appointments	Expenses	Appointments	Expenses
29 Monday 2pm Weston Products - visit new site at Twyford	Mileage?	2 Friday 9am Interviews at Head Office - all day	
30 Tuesday 9am Head Office 1pm - Coates Ltd at Salisbury Discuss new range - Lunch Overnight	Lunch £60 Mileage? Hotel £90	3 Saturday	
31 Wednesday Drive to Southampton - Brown & Co On to Universal Products at Oxford Overnight	Mileage? Mileage? Hotel £62	4 Sunday	
1 Thursday 12 noon - Hoe Products at Plymouth 1pm Lunch Return to Head Office	Mileage? Lunch £52 Mileage?		

Fig 4.10 Diary page

Payments:

- check statements against invoices and credit notes for payment authorisation
- check expenses claim forms for staff against approved allowances for payment authorisation
- complete cheques ready for signature and remittance advices
- complete documentation for payment by credit transfers

Assess your work in these tasks against the following NVQ performance criteria

ELEMENT 7.2   Prepare a variety of documents
(Level 2)

Performance criteria
a Instructions are understood.
b Completed documentation meets the requirements of the workplace.

c Layout, spelling, grammar and punctuation are consistent and in accordance with conventions and house style.
d Corrections, when appropriate, are unobtrusive.
e Security and confidentiality of information is maintained.
f Copies and originals are correctly collated and routed, as directed.
g Where work is not achievable within specified deadlines reasons are promptly and accurately reported.
h Work is achieved within agreed deadlines.

ELEMENT 10.2   Process claims for payment
(Level 2)

Performance criteria
a Claims are verified in accordance with organisational procedures.
b Computations are checked for accuracy and validity.

c Discrepancies are investigated and resolved within own authority or referred to an appropriate authority.

d Referral of verified claims to appropriate others is in accordance with organisational procedures.

e Records are accurate, complete and legible.

Unit 5
Petty cash

1 Amanda Jackson keeps a petty cash account for sundry items of expenditure which she has to make on behalf of Compton Community Association. She begins the month of January with an imprest of £50 out of which she has to make the following cash purchases:

		£
5 Jan	postage stamps	5.00
12 Jan	copier paper	6.00
14 Jan	telephone calls	1.45
19 Jan	table tennis balls	2.42
26 Jan	two cassettes for recorder	10.50
28 Jan	gift voucher	10.00
29 Jan	telephone calls	0.80
31 Jan	postal order	2.20

Complete petty cash vouchers for each of these items and enter them in a petty cash account for January, allocating appropriate analysis columns. Total the columns, balance the account and restore the imprest on 1 February.

2 In this assignment you are employed by R W Fothergill & Co to assist Luke McCabe, the accounts clerk. At the beginning of the month of June you are allocated an imprest of £50 by Mr P Green, the cashier. Using the petty cash vouchers in Fig 5.1, complete the petty cash account for the month, allocating appropriate analysis columns for the needs of the office. Total the columns, balance the account and restore the imprest on 1 July.

3 Naomi Tilling, cashier at Systems Furniture plc, who normally deals with the petty cash, is away ill and you have been asked to deal with it until she returns. She has partly completed the petty cash account for June.
a Check her entries in the petty cash account in Fig 5.2 and if you discover any errors correct them and re-write the account.

b You were asked to make the following cash purchases during the final week of June:

23 June thirty first class postage stamps
24 June a copy of *The Financial Times*
26 June a postal order for 75p
27 June two ring binders £8.50 plus VAT

Verify and calculate the amounts and complete petty cash vouchers for them.
c Enter the petty cash vouchers in the account, total and balance it, and restore the imprest on 1 July.

4 You are in charge of your company's petty cash account which is kept on the imprest system. From the petty cash vouchers in Fig 5.4 complete the last six transactions for April in the petty cash book in Fig 5.3. Total the columns, balance the book and restore the imprest.

5 Each petty cash voucher in Fig 5.5 has been allocated a letter. The Petty Cashier has refused to accept the three vouchers labelled A, C and E.
a Write the letter allocated to each incorrect voucher and state the error involved. In each case give one reason why the Petty Cashier has refused to accept the voucher.
b Allocate a number to each of the correct vouchers and using only these vouchers complete the petty cash book in Fig 5.6. Total and balance the book as at 22 June 19– and restore the imprest.
c List two precautions to be taken to safeguard the petty cash box.
d State the department responsible for administering the petty cash system.

Petty Cash Voucher	No _1_ Date 2 June 19–		
		Amount	
For what required		£	p
Postage stamps		8	00
		8	00
Signature J. Bates			
Passed by P. Green			

Petty Cash Voucher	No _2_ Date 3 June 19–		
		Amount	
For what required		£	p
Magazines for waiting room		2	25
		2	25
Signature G. Street			
Passed by P. Green			

Petty Cash Voucher	No _3_ Date 4 June 19–		
		Amount	
For what required		£	p
"Get well" card		1	20
		1	20
Signature P. Whitehead			
Passed by P. Green			

Petty Cash Voucher	No _4_ Date 9 June 19–		
		Amount	
For what required		£	p
Registered post		3	25
		3	25
Signature J. Bates			
Passed by P. Green			

Petty Cash Voucher	No _5_ Date 16 June 19–		
		Amount	
For what required		£	p
Two Boxes of address labels		5	20
plus VAT		–	91
		6	11
Signature G. Street			
Passed by P. Green			

Petty Cash Voucher	No _6_ Date 23 June 19–		
		Amount	
For what required		£	p
Taxi fares		5	25
		5	25
Signature J. Bates			
Passed by P. Green			

Petty Cash Voucher	No _7_ Date 24 June 19–		
		Amount	
For what required		£	p
Packet of 10 stamped Royal Mail envelopes		2	70
		2	70
Signature P. Whitehead			
Passed by P. Green			

Petty Cash Voucher	No _8_ Date 29 June 19–		
		Amount	
For what required		£	p
4 rolls of sellotape		10	–
plus VAT		1	75
		11	75
Signature J. Bates			
Passed by P. Green			

Fig 5.1

Received		Date 19--	Particulars	Fo	V No	Total paid out		Stationery	Office expenses		Travelling		Postage		VAT	
			SYSTEMS FURNITURE plc													
Dr			PETTY CASH ACCOUNT											Cr		
30	00	June 1	Balance b/d													
20	00	" 1	Cash received	CB1												
		" 2	Postage stamps		70	3	00				3	00				
		" 4	Window cleaning		71	10	50		10	50						
		" 8	Railway ticket		72	2	45		2	45						
		" 9	Jar of coffee		73	2	10		2	10						
		" 15	Postal order		74	1	65						1	65		
		" 17	Envelopes (inc VAT)		75	5	00		5	00					0	88

Fig 5.2

Received		Date 19--	Details	V No	Total paid out		Postage		Travelling		Cleaning		Sundry expenses		VAT	
Dr			PETTY CASH ACCOUNT												Cr	
50	00	1 4	Cash													
		3 4	Washing up liquid	1	0	94					0	80			0	14
		7 4	Registered letter	2	3	25	3	25								
		10 4	Window cleaning	3	9	40					8	00			1	40
		13 4	Taxi	4	5	00			5	00						

Fig 5.3

40

Petty Cash Voucher	No 5 Date 16/4 19–		
		Amount	
For what required		£	p
Stamps		6	00
		6	00
Signature M. Atkinson			
Passed by P. A. Hirst			

Petty Cash Voucher	No 6 Date 16/4 19–		
		Amount	
For what required		£	p
Instant coffee		2	35
		2	35
Signature J. Morgan			
Passed by P. A. Hirst			

Petty Cash Voucher	No 7 Date 17/4 19–		
		Amount	
For what required		£	p
Adhesive tape			80
VAT			14
			94
Signature B. Arnold			
Passed by P. A. Hirst			

Petty Cash Voucher	No 8 Date 20/4 19–		
		Amount	
For what required		£	p
Fares		1	25
		1	25
Signature B. Arnold			
Passed by P. A. Hirst			

Petty Cash Voucher	No 9 Date 23/4 19–		
		Amount	
For what required		£	p
Stationery		3	15
VAT			55
		3	70
Signature J. Morgan			
Passed by P. A. Hirst			

Petty Cash Voucher	No 10 Date 27/4 19–		
		Amount	
For what required		£	p
Plasters		1	10
		1	10
Signature D. Pinner			
Passed by P. A. Hirst			

Fig 5.4

A

Petty Cash Voucher
No _____ Date 22/6 19–

For what required	Amount £	p
	7	85
	7	85

Signature _____ P Jenkins

Passed by _____ Adrian Bird

B

Petty Cash Voucher
No _____ Date 22/6 19–

For what required	Amount £	p
White erasing fluid	1	17
(inc VAT 17p)		
	1	17

Signature _____ H. Hill

Passed by _____ Adrian Bird

C

Petty Cash Voucher
No _____ Date 22 June 19–

For what required	Amount £	p
Biscuits	1	98
Coffee	2	45
	4	43

Signature _____

Passed by _____ Adrian Bird

D

Petty Cash Voucher
No _____ Date 22.6 19–

For what required	Amount £	p
C.O.D.	4	85
	4	85

Signature _____ R. Rose

Passed by _____ Adrian Bird

E

Petty Cash Voucher
No _____ Date _____ 19–

For what required	Amount £	p
Stamps	10	00
	10	00

Signature _____ S. Abbott

Passed by _____ Adrian Bird

F

Petty Cash Voucher
No _____ Date 22/4 19–

For what required	Amount £	p
Fabric Plaster	2	70

Signature _____ F. Jarvis

Passed by _____ Adrian Bird

Fig 5.5

Dr					PETTY CASH BOOK								Cr
Received		Date	Details	V No	Total paid out		Postage		Office expenses		Travel	Stationery	VAT
10	80	June 01	Balance b/f										
89	20	" 01	Cash received										
		" 03	Printer ribbons	87	23	26						19 80	3 46
		" 05	Milk	88	2	10			2	10			
		" 09	Stamps	89	5	00	5	00					
		" 12	Milk	90	2	10			2	10			
		" 17	Underground ticket	91	2	80					2 80		
		" 19	Milk	92	2	32			2	32			

Fig 5.6

6 Last week the petty cash book did not balance. Mr Palmer, the Chief Cashier, is sure that the money was not stolen, and believes that petty cash vouchers were not completed for each purchase made.

a Draft a memo to be sent by Mr Palmer to all Heads of Department,
  i informing them of what has happened
  ii reminding them of the purpose of the petty cash voucher
  iii pointing out their responsibility in ensuring that items bought on behalf of the firm must be authorised and monitored.
b State five precautions which the petty cashier should follow to make sure that the cash in the office is kept secure.
c Explain what is meant by the expression 'the petty cash book did not balance'.

7 Assume that one of your responsibilities is to handle the petty cash requirements of your office. You are given £25 to use for the imprest. Complete and balance a Petty Cash Book from the vouchers in Fig 5.7, also taking account of

the following two additional items:
a a receipt for £4.50 for a taxi fare which a member of staff incurred when asked to deliver an urgent package to a client (10 September).
b £3.20 in cash which was given by a client who made a long distance telephone call from your office (20 September), and restore the Imprest on 1 October.

8 You have been asked to train a colleague who is to take responsibility for the Petty Cash in your office. It is kept on the Imprest System.
a Give a detailed explanation of how this system operates.
b State two ways in which the security of cash can be ensured.

(PQ OP1)

9 The company has decided to reorganise the petty cash system using the Imprest system and you have been asked to be responsible for this. Your float is £50 per month. At the end of the first month (April) you have paid out cash in

| PETTY CASH VOUCHER | Voucher 17 |
| Date 8/9 |

For what required	AMOUNT £ p
Flowers for Reception	6 70
	6 70

Signed A B Johns

Passed by AD

| PETTY CASH VOUCHER | Voucher 18 |
| Date 14/9 |

For what required	AMOUNT £ p
Postage stamps etc	2 78
	6 65

Signed J B Winston

Passed by AD

| PETTY CASH VOUCHER | Voucher 19 |
| Date 16/9 |

For what required	AMOUNT £ p
Coffee and sugar	2 65
	2 65

Signed N T Sakirk

Passed by AD

| PETTY CASH VOUCHER | Voucher 20 |
| Date 20/9 |

For what required	AMOUNT £ p
Magic markers Glue stick	1 48 / 70
	2 18

Signed S R Phillips

Passed by AD

Fig 5.7

accordance with the petty cash vouchers (Fig 5.8). Complete and balance the attached petty cash account sheet as at 1 May showing the amount you receive from the Cashier to restore the imprest.

(PQ OP1)

▶ **COMPUTER/WP TASKS**

10 Use a spreadsheet package to calculate the total and individual petty cash expenses for:
a the current year from the data supplied from

the petty cash book in Fig 5.9.
b next year having regard to the following pre-dicted adjustments:
  i an inflationary increase of 5% for sta-tionery, cleaning and sundry expenses;
  ii an inflationary increase of 7.5% for trav-elling expenses;
  iii an increase of 4% for postage costs with effect from 1 July when higher postal charges are expected to be introduced.
Print out both spreadsheets and save the final copies on disk.
c Use a word processor to prepare a memo

Petty Cash Voucher		Voucher _1_
		Date _3 April_
For what required	£	p
Large manilla envelopes	5	20
	5	20
Signature Paul Collar		
Passed by Rg		

Petty Cash Voucher		Voucher _3_
		Date _9 April_
For what required	£	p
Taxi fare to airport	10	50
	10	50
Signature S. Cushing		
Passed by Rg		

Petty Cash Voucher		Voucher _2_
		Date _7 April_
For what required	£	p
Stamps	13	85
	13	85
Signature M Smith		
Passed by PB		

Petty Cash Voucher		Voucher _4_
		Date _17 April_
For what required	£	p
Gummed labels		75
		75
Signature RP Blitz		
Passed by Rg		

Petty Cash Voucher		Voucher _5_
		Date _24 April_
For what required	£	p
Supplies for first aid box	8	25
	8	25
Signature D Brown		
Passed by PB		

Petty Cash Voucher		Voucher _6_
		Date _25 April_
For what required	£	p
Window Cleaning	4	00
	4	00
Signature Jane Brown		
Passed by PB		

Fig 5.8

from the Chief Cashier to the Petty Cashier incorporating the totals from both spread-sheets and explaining the basis on which the predictions have been made. Say that the estimates must not be exceeded.

► **WORK EXPERIENCE TASKS**

11 Work in the cashier's section:

● take charge of the petty cash system, receiving cash from the cashier and paying out money in return for receipts and vouchers
● file receipts and vouchers

PETTY CASH EXPENDITURE TOTALS FOR THE YEAR 19--

Month	Stationery £	Postage £	Travelling £	Cleaning £	Sundry £	Totals £
Jan.	6.24	15.00	18.20	8.50	4.20	
Feb.	7.82	14.80	22.19	6.50	5.78	
March	14.10	13.40	15.35	4.56	6.42	
April	9.60	12.60	17.50	7.60	9.10	
May	20.50	13.90	14.00	3.88	8.20	
June	8.40	15.00	15.40	5.00	5.15	
July	12.50	17.00	16.30	7.35	8.43	
Aug.	10.50	18.40	19.00	3.60	8.30	
Sept.	9.95	17.50	14.25	4.00	10.20	
Oct.	8.95	18.12	17.50	8.50	9.10	
Nov.	11.30	18.50	15.28	5.00	9.99	
Dec.	18.40	17.35	16.40	7.70	6.50	
TOTALS						

Fig 5.9

Assess your work in these tasks against the following NVQ performance criteria

ELEMENT 5.3   Check and process routine numerical information
(Level 1)

Performance criteria
a Numerical information is checked accurately.
b Inconsistencies are promptly reported to the appropriate person.
c The recording and processing of checked, numerical information is carried out as instructed.

ELEMENT 10.2   Process claims for payment
(Level 2)

Performance criteria
a Claims are verified in accordance with organisational procedures.
b Computations are checked for accuracy and validity.
c Discrepancies are investigated and resolved within own authority or referred to an appropriate authority.
d Referral of verified claims to appropriate others is in accordance with organisational procedures.
e Records are accurate, complete and legible.

Unit 6
Wages and salaries

Paul Prince, wages clerk at Systems Furniture plc, is on a week's holiday and you have been transferred to his office to assist in the preparation of the pay for the weekly paid employees.

1 Calculate the gross wages for three employees – C Green, R Page and R Southern – from the clock cards in Fig 6.1 for week 3.

2 Using the information in 1 and the income tax tables (Figs 6.2 and 6.3) and NI tables (Fig 6.4), complete income tax deductions working sheets for each of these employees for week 3. The employees pay 5% of their salary into a pension fund which is deducted from gross pay before calculating income tax. Begin by entering the week 2 entries which are illustrated in Fig 6.5.

3 Complete pay advice slips for each of these employees. Their voluntary deductions are as follows:

	Savings	Social fund
C Green	£1.00	£1.00
R Southern	£2.50	£1.00
R Page	£5.00	£1.00

4 Naomi Tilling calls in to the wages office to query the amount of income tax which has been deducted in week 2. She says that it is more than last week for the same amount of gross pay. Check her deductions working sheet (Fig 6.6) with the tax tables and if an error has been made correct it and re-write the deductions working sheet. What circumstances might have resulted in Naomi having to pay more tax without an increase in wages?

5

a Prepare a payroll (as illustrated on page 150) for the following employees of Systems Furniture plc for Week 3 based on the data supplied and the income tax tables (Figs 6.2 and 6.3) and NI tables (Fig 6.4):

Employee	Tax Code	Total Gross Pay up to Wk 2	Tax paid up to Wk 2	Gross Pay in Wk 3	Other Deductions
		£	£	£	£
R O'Brien	528H	540.00	77.84	280.00	7.00
A T Palliser	352L	360.00	49.84	180.00	4.00
P Patel	400L	440.00	65.09	200.00	5.00
P Prince	380L	370.00	49.59	190.00	3.00
T A Redpath	548H	480.00	63.34	250.00	8.00

b Except for Mr Palliser who is paid by cheque, the rest of the staff are paid in cash.
   i   Complete a cheque to pay Mr Palliser his wages
   ii For the other four members of staff complete a coining analysis and cash summary, using the information from the payroll.

c Mrs O'Brien is leaving this week to work for another company:
   i   Name the tax document which she must be given when she leaves Systems Furniture plc.
   ii State the procedure which Systems Furniture plc must follow with this document.
   iii State the procedure Mrs O'Brien must follow with the document and explain why it is important to her.

CLOCK CARD

No 97   Name: R SOUTHERN

Week ending: 26 April 19--   Week No 3

Day	In	Out	In	Out	TOTAL HOURS
M	0801	1301	1401	1701	
Tu	0759	1300	1400	1700	
W	0756	1300	1401	1700	
Th	0800	1259	1359	1601	
F	0801	1300	1400	1600	
TOTAL					

Ordinary time:.........hrs @ £6.00
(up to 38 hours)

Overtime:.............hrs @ £9.00

TOTAL GROSS WAGES

CLOCK CARD

No 95   Name: C GREEN

Week ending: 26 April 19--   Week No 3

Day	In	Out	In	Out	TOTAL HOURS
M	0801	1202	1300	1700	
Tu	0759	1200	1300	1700	
W	0802	1202	1301	1659	
Th	0801	1203	1258	1700	
F	0800	1201	1300	1600	
TOTAL					

Ordinary time:.........hrs @ £5.20
(up to 38 hours)

Overtime:.............hrs @ £7.80

TOTAL GROSS WAGES

CLOCK CARD

No 96   Name: R PAGE

Week ending: 26 April 19--   Week No 3

Day	In	Out	In	Out	TOTAL HOURS
M	0800	1301	1400	1700	
Tu	0756	1300	1358	1656	
W	0759	1301	1400	1701	
Th	0800	1302	1401	1804	
F	0801	1300	1400	1701	
TOTAL					

Ordinary time:.........hrs @ £5.60
(up to 38 hours)

Overtime:.............hrs @ £8.40   £

TOTAL GROSS WAGES

Fig 6.1

TABLE A - PAY ADJUSTMENT

Week 2
Apr 13 to Apr 19

Code	Total pay adjustment to date £	Code	Total pay adjustment to date £	Code	Total pay adjustment to date £	Code	Total pay adjustment to date £	Code	Total pay adjustment to date £	Code	Total pay adjustment to date £	Code	Total pay adjustment to date £	Code	Total pay adjustment to date £	Code	Total pay adjustment to date £
0	NIL																
1	0.74	61	23.82	121	46.90	181	69.98	241	93.04	301	116.12	351	135.36	401	154.58	451	173.82
2	1.12	62	24.20	122	47.28	182	70.36	242	93.44	302	116.50	352	135.74	402	154.98	452	174.20
3	1.50	63	24.58	123	47.66	183	70.74	243	93.82	303	116.90	353	136.12	403	155.36	453	174.58
4	1.90	64	24.98	124	48.04	184	71.12	244	94.20	304	117.28	354	136.50	404	155.74	454	174.98
5	2.28	65	25.36	125	48.44	185	71.50	245	94.58	305	117.66	355	136.90	405	156.12	455	175.36
6	2.66	66	25.74	126	48.82	186	71.90	246	94.98	306	118.04	356	137.28	406	156.50	456	175.74
7	3.04	67	26.12	127	49.20	187	72.28	247	95.36	307	118.44	357	137.66	407	156.90	457	176.12
8	3.44	68	26.50	128	49.58	188	72.66	248	95.74	308	118.82	358	138.04	408	157.28	458	176.50
9	3.82	69	26.90	129	49.98	189	73.04	249	96.12	309	119.20	359	138.44	409	157.66	459	176.90
10	4.20	70	27.28	130	50.36	190	73.44	250	96.50	310	119.58	360	138.82	410	158.04	460	177.28
11	4.58	71	27.66	131	50.74	191	73.82	251	96.90	311	119.98	361	139.20	411	158.44	461	177.66
12	4.98	72	28.04	132	51.12	192	74.20	252	97.28	312	120.36	362	139.58	412	158.82	462	178.04
13	5.36	73	28.44	133	51.50	193	74.58	253	97.66	313	120.74	363	139.98	413	159.20	463	178.44
14	5.74	74	28.82	134	51.90	194	74.98	254	98.04	314	121.12	364	140.36	414	159.58	464	178.82
15	6.12	75	29.20	135	52.28	195	75.36	255	98.44	315	121.50	365	140.74	415	159.98	465	179.20
16	6.50	76	29.58	136	52.66	196	75.74	256	98.82	316	121.90	366	141.12	416	160.36	466	179.58
17	6.90	77	29.98	137	53.04	197	76.12	257	99.20	317	122.28	367	141.50	417	160.74	467	179.98
18	7.28	78	30.36	138	53.44	198	76.50	258	99.58	318	122.66	368	141.90	418	161.12	468	180.36
19	7.66	79	30.74	139	53.82	199	76.90	259	99.98	319	123.04	369	142.28	419	161.50	469	180.74
20	8.04	80	31.12	140	54.20	200	77.28	260	100.36	320	123.44	370	142.66	420	161.90	470	181.12
21	8.44	81	31.50	141	54.58	201	77.66	261	100.74	321	123.82	371	143.04	421	162.28	471	181.50
22	8.82	82	31.90	142	54.98	202	78.04	262	101.12	322	124.20	372	143.44	422	162.66	472	181.90
23	9.20	83	32.28	143	55.36	203	78.44	263	101.50	323	124.58	373	143.82	423	163.04	473	182.28
24	9.58	84	32.66	144	55.74	204	78.82	264	101.90	324	124.98	374	144.20	424	163.44	474	182.66
25	9.98	85	33.04	145	56.12	205	79.20	265	102.28	325	125.36	375	144.58	425	163.82	475	183.04
26	10.36	86	33.44	146	56.50	206	79.58	266	102.66	326	125.74	376	144.98	426	164.20	476	183.44
27	10.74	87	33.82	147	56.90	207	79.98	267	103.04	327	126.12	377	145.36	427	164.58	477	183.82
28	11.12	88	34.20	148	57.28	208	80.36	268	103.44	328	126.50	378	145.74	428	164.98	478	184.20
29	11.50	89	34.58	149	57.66	209	80.74	269	103.84	329	126.90	379	146.12	429	165.36	479	184.58
30	11.90	90	34.98	150	58.04	210	81.12	270	104.20	330	127.28	380	146.50	430	165.74	480	184.98
31	12.28	91	35.36	151	58.44	211	81.50	271	104.58	331	127.66	381	146.90	431	166.12	481	185.36
32	12.66	92	35.74	152	58.82	212	81.90	272	104.98	332	128.04	382	147.28	432	166.50	482	185.74
33	13.04	93	36.12	153	59.20	213	82.28	273	105.36	333	128.44	383	147.66	433	166.90	483	186.12
34	13.44	94	36.50	154	59.58	214	82.66	274	105.74	334	128.82	384	148.04	434	167.28	484	186.50
35	13.82	95	36.90	155	59.98	215	83.04	275	106.12	335	129.20	385	148.44	435	167.66	485	186.90
36	14.20	96	37.28	156	60.36	216	83.44	276	106.50	336	129.58	386	148.82	436	168.04	486	187.28
37	14.58	97	37.66	157	60.74	217	83.82	277	106.90	337	129.98	387	149.20	437	168.44	487	187.66
38	14.98	98	38.04	158	61.12	218	84.20	278	107.28	338	130.36	388	149.58	438	168.82	488	188.04
39	15.36	99	38.44	159	61.50	219	84.58	279	107.66	339	130.74	389	149.98	439	169.20	489	188.44
40	15.74	100	38.82	160	61.90	220	84.98	280	108.04	340	131.12	390	150.36	440	169.58	490	188.82
41	16.12	101	39.20	161	62.28	221	85.36	281	108.44	341	131.50	391	150.74	441	169.98	491	189.20
42	16.50	102	39.58	162	62.66	222	85.74	282	108.82	342	131.90	392	151.12	442	170.36	492	189.58
43	16.90	103	39.98	163	63.04	223	86.12	283	109.20	343	132.28	393	151.50	443	170.74	493	189.98
44	17.28	104	40.36	164	63.44	224	86.50	284	109.58	344	132.66	394	151.90	444	171.12	494	190.36
45	17.66	105	40.74	165	63.82	225	86.90	285	109.98	345	133.04	395	152.28	445	171.50	495	190.74
46	18.04	106	41.12	166	64.20	226	87.28	286	110.36	346	133.44	396	152.66	446	171.90	496	191.12
47	18.44	107	41.50	167	64.58	227	87.66	287	110.74	347	133.82	397	153.04	447	172.28	497	191.50
48	18.82	108	41.90	168	64.98	228	88.04	288	111.12	348	134.20	398	153.44	448	172.66	498	191.90
49	19.20	109	42.28	169	65.36	229	88.44	289	111.50	349	134.58	399	153.82	449	173.04	499	192.28
50	19.58	110	42.66	170	65.74	230	88.82	290	111.90	350	134.98	400	154.20	450	173.44	500	192.66
51	19.98	111	43.04	171	66.12	231	89.20	291	112.28								
52	20.36	112	43.44	172	66.50	232	89.58	292	112.66								
53	20.74	113	43.82	173	66.90	233	89.98	293	113.04								
54	21.12	114	44.20	174	67.28	234	90.36	294	113.44								
55	21.50	115	44.58	175	67.66	235	90.74	295	113.82								
56	21.90	116	44.98	176	68.04	236	91.12	296	114.20								
57	22.28	117	45.36	177	68.44	237	91.50	297	114.58								
58	22.66	118	45.74	178	68.82	238	91.90	298	114.98								
59	23.04	119	46.12	179	69.20	239	92.28	299	115.36								
60	23.44	120	46.50	180	69.58	240	92.66	300	115.74								

Pay adjustment where code exceeds 500

1. Where the code is in the range **501** to **1000** inclusive proceed as follows:

   a. Subtract **500** from the code and use the balance of the code to obtain a pay adjustment figure from the table above.

   b. Add this pay adjustment figure to the figure given in the box alongside to obtain the figure of total pay adjustment to date * **£192.32**

2. Where the code **exceeds 1000** follow the instructions on **page 2**.

4

Fig 6.2 (Crown copyright)

Pages 2 and 3 tell you when to use these tables

Table B
(Tax at 25%)

Remember to use the Subtraction Tables on Page 7

Tax Due on Taxable Pay from £1 to £99

Total TAXABLE PAY to date (£)	Total TAX DUE to date (£)	Total TAXABLE PAY to date (£)	Total TAX DUE to date (£)
1	0.25	61	15.25
2	0.50	62	15.50
3	0.75	63	15.75
4	1.00	64	16.00
5	1.25	65	16.25
6	1.50	66	16.50
7	1.75	67	16.75
8	2.00	68	17.00
9	2.25	69	17.25
10	2.50	70	17.50
11	2.75	71	17.75
12	3.00	72	18.00
13	3.25	73	18.25
14	3.50	74	18.50
15	3.75	75	18.75
16	4.00	76	19.00
17	4.25	77	19.25
18	4.50	78	19.50
19	4.75	79	19.75
20	5.00	80	20.00
21	5.25	81	20.25
22	5.50	82	20.50
23	5.75	83	20.75
24	6.00	84	21.00
25	6.25	85	21.25
26	6.50	86	21.50
27	6.75	87	21.75
28	7.00	88	22.00
29	7.25	89	22.25
30	7.50	90	22.50
31	7.75	91	22.75
32	8.00	92	23.00
33	8.25	93	23.25
34	8.50	94	23.50
35	8.75	95	23.75
36	9.00	96	24.00
37	9.25	97	24.25
38	9.50	98	24.50
39	9.75	99	24.75
40	10.00		
41	10.25		
42	10.50		
43	10.75		
44	11.00		
45	11.25		
46	11.50		
47	11.75		
48	12.00		
49	12.25		
50	12.50		
51	12.75		
52	13.00		
53	13.25		
54	13.50		
55	13.75		
56	14.00		
57	14.25		
58	14.50		
59	14.75		
60	15.00		

Tax Due on Taxable Pay from £100 to £24,300

TAXABLE PAY (£)	TAX DUE (£)	TAXABLE PAY (£)	TAX DUE (£)	TAXABLE PAY (£)	TAX DUE (£)	TAXABLE PAY (£)	TAX DUE (£)
100	25.00	6100	1525.00	12100	3025.00	18100	4525.00
200	50.00	6200	1550.00	12200	3050.00	18200	4550.00
300	75.00	6300	1575.00	12300	3075.00	18300	4575.00
400	100.00	6400	1600.00	12400	3100.00	18400	4600.00
500	125.00	6500	1625.00	12500	3125.00	18500	4625.00
600	150.00	6600	1650.00	12600	3150.00	18600	4650.00
700	175.00	6700	1675.00	12700	3175.00	18700	4675.00
800	200.00	6800	1700.00	12800	3200.00	18800	4700.00
900	225.00	6900	1725.00	12900	3225.00	18900	4725.00
1000	250.00	7000	1750.00	13000	3250.00	19000	4750.00
1100	275.00	7100	1775.00	13100	3275.00	19100	4775.00
1200	300.00	7200	1800.00	13200	3300.00	19200	4800.00
1300	325.00	7300	1825.00	13300	3325.00	19300	4825.00
1400	350.00	7400	1850.00	13400	3350.00	19400	4850.00
1500	375.00	7500	1875.00	13500	3375.00	19500	4875.00
1600	400.00	7600	1900.00	13600	3400.00	19600	4900.00
1700	425.00	7700	1925.00	13700	3425.00	19700	4925.00
1800	450.00	7800	1950.00	13800	3450.00	19800	4950.00
1900	475.00	7900	1975.00	13900	3475.00	19900	4975.00
2000	500.00	8000	2000.00	14000	3500.00	20000	5000.00
2100	525.00	8100	2025.00	14100	3525.00	20100	5025.00
2200	550.00	8200	2050.00	14200	3550.00	20200	5050.00
2300	575.00	8300	2075.00	14300	3575.00	20300	5075.00
2400	600.00	8400	2100.00	14400	3600.00	20400	5100.00
2500	625.00	8500	2125.00	14500	3625.00	20500	5125.00
2600	650.00	8600	2150.00	14600	3650.00	20600	5150.00
2700	675.00	8700	2175.00	14700	3675.00	20700	5175.00
2800	700.00	8800	2200.00	14800	3700.00	20800	5200.00
2900	725.00	8900	2225.00	14900	3725.00	20900	5225.00
3000	750.00	9000	2250.00	15000	3750.00	21000	5250.00
3100	775.00	9100	2275.00	15100	3775.00	21100	5275.00
3200	800.00	9200	2300.00	15200	3800.00	21200	5300.00
3300	825.00	9300	2325.00	15300	3825.00	21300	5325.00
3400	850.00	9400	2350.00	15400	3850.00	21400	5350.00
3500	875.00	9500	2375.00	15500	3875.00	21500	5375.00
3600	900.00	9600	2400.00	15600	3900.00	21600	5400.00
3700	925.00	9700	2425.00	15700	3925.00	21700	5425.00
3800	950.00	9800	2450.00	15800	3950.00	21800	5450.00
3900	975.00	9900	2475.00	15900	3975.00	21900	5475.00
4000	1000.00	10000	2500.00	16000	4000.00	22000	5500.00
4100	1025.00	10100	2525.00	16100	4025.00	22100	5525.00
4200	1050.00	10200	2550.00	16200	4050.00	22200	5550.00
4300	1075.00	10300	2575.00	16300	4075.00	22300	5575.00
4400	1100.00	10400	2600.00	16400	4100.00	22400	5600.00
4500	1125.00	10500	2625.00	16500	4125.00	22500	5625.00
4600	1150.00	10600	2650.00	16600	4150.00	22600	5650.00
4700	1175.00	10700	2675.00	16700	4175.00	22700	5675.00
4800	1200.00	10800	2700.00	16800	4200.00	22800	5700.00
4900	1225.00	10900	2725.00	16900	4225.00	22900	5725.00
5000	1250.00	11000	2750.00	17000	4250.00	23000	5750.00
5100	1275.00	11100	2775.00	17100	4275.00	23100	5775.00
5200	1300.00	11200	2800.00	17200	4300.00	23200	5800.00
5300	1325.00	11300	2825.00	17300	4325.00	23300	5825.00
5400	1350.00	11400	2850.00	17400	4350.00	23400	5850.00
5500	1375.00	11500	2875.00	17500	4375.00	23500	5875.00
5600	1400.00	11600	2900.00	17600	4400.00	23600	5900.00
5700	1425.00	11700	2925.00	17700	4425.00	23700	5925.00
5800	1450.00	11800	2950.00	17800	4450.00	23800	5950.00
5900	1475.00	11900	2975.00	17900	4475.00	23900	5975.00
6000	1500.00	12000	3000.00	18000	4500.00	24000	6000.00
						24100	6025.00
						24200	6050.00
						24300	6075.00

Where the exact amount of taxable pay is not shown, add together the figures for two (or more) entries to make up the amount of taxable pay to the nearest £1 below

6

Remember to use the Subtraction Tables on Page 7

Fig 6.3(a) (Crown copyright)

Table B Subtraction Tables
(Lower Rate Relief)

Do not use the subtraction tables for code BR

For all ordinary suffix codes and prefix K codes - When you have used the table on Page 6
to work out the tax at 25% refer to the tables below to give the benefit of
the lower rate band. Find the week or month in which the pay day falls.
(it is the same week or month you have used in Tables A) and **subtract**
the amount shown to arrive at the tax due.
There is an example below and further examples on Page 8

Employee paid at Weekly rates

Week No.	Amount to subtract £
1	3.08
2	6.16
3	9.24
4	12.31
5	15.39
6	18.47
7	21.54
8	24.62
9	27.70
10	30.77
11	33.85
12	36.93
13	40.00
14	43.08
15	46.16
16	49.24
17	52.31
18	55.39
19	58.47
20	61.54
21	64.62
22	67.70
23	70.77
24	73.85
25	76.93
26	80.00
27	83.08
28	86.16
29	89.24
30	92.31
31	95.39
32	98.47
33	101.54
34	104.62
35	107.70
36	110.77
37	113.85
38	116.93
39	120.00
40	123.08
41	126.16
42	129.24
43	132.31
44	135.39
45	138.47
46	141.54
47	144.62
48	147.70
49	150.77
50	153.85
51	156.93
52	160.00

Employee paid at Monthly rates

Month No.	Amount to subtract
1	13.34
2	26.67
3	40.00
4	53.34
5	66.67
6	80.00
7	93.34
8	106.67
9	120.00
10	133.34
11	146.67
12	160.00

Use of Table B   *Example 1*

Employee's code is **352L**
The payment is made in **Week 7**

Pay in the week	£ 200
Previous pay to date	£1200
Total pay to date	£1400
Less free pay in Week 7 (from Table A)	£ 475.09
Total taxable pay to date	**£ 924.91**

The tax is worked out by first looking in Table B on Page 6
for the nearest round figure below £924

		Tax due
It is	£900	£225.00
Look in the shaded columns for the remainder	£ 24	£ 6.00
Totals	£924	£231.00

*Then give the Lower Rate Relief by
looking in the table on this page for
Week 7 and subtract the amount
from the tax due. It is*   £ 21.54

Total tax due to date   **£209.46**

7

Fig 6.3(b) (Crown copyright)

6 April 1995 to 5 April 1996   **A**

Weekly table for not contracted-out standard rate contributions

Use this table for:

- employees who are over age 16 and under pension age

- employees who have an Appropriate Personal Pension

Do not use this table for:

- married women and widows who pay reduced rate National Insurance contributions

- employees who are over pension age

- employees for whom you hold form RD950

Completing form P11:

- enter 'A' in the space provided on the Deductions Working Sheet P11 or substitute

- copy the figures in columns 1a, 1b and 1c to columns 1a, 1b and 1c of form P11

If the exact gross pay is not shown in the table, use the next smaller figure shown.

Earnings on which employee's contributions payable 1a	Total of employee's and employer's contributions payable 1b	Employee's contributions payable 1c	Employer's contributions*	Earnings on which employee's contributions payable 1a	Total of employee's and employer's contributions payable 1b	Employee's contributions payable 1c	Employer's contributions*
£	£	£	£	£	£	£	£
58	2.90	1.16	1.74	98	8.16	5.21	2.95
59	3.09	1.31	1.78	99	8.29	5.31	2.98
60	3.22	1.41	1.81	100	8.42	5.41	3.01
61	3.35	1.51	1.84	101	8.55	5.51	3.04
62	3.48	1.61	1.87	102	8.68	5.61	3.07
63	3.61	1.71	1.90	103	8.81	5.71	3.10
64	3.74	1.81	1.93	104	8.94	5.81	3.13
65	3.87	1.91	1.96	105	11.18	5.91	5.27
66	4.00	2.01	1.99	106	11.33	6.01	5.32
67	4.13	2.11	2.02	107	11.48	6.11	5.37
68	4.26	2.21	2.05	108	11.63	6.21	5.42
69	4.39	2.31	2.08	109	11.78	6.31	5.47
70	4.52	2.41	2.11	110	11.93	6.41	5.52
71	4.65	2.51	2.14	111	12.08	6.51	5.57
72	4.78	2.61	2.17	112	12.23	6.61	5.62
73	4.91	2.71	2.20	113	12.38	6.71	5.67
74	5.04	2.81	2.23	114	12.53	6.81	5.72
75	5.17	2.91	2.26	115	12.68	6.91	5.77
76	5.30	3.01	2.29	116	12.83	7.01	5.82
77	5.43	3.11	2.32	117	12.98	7.11	5.87
78	5.56	3.21	2.35	118	13.13	7.21	5.92
79	5.69	3.31	2.38	119	13.28	7.31	5.97
80	5.82	3.41	2.41	120	13.43	7.41	6.02
81	5.95	3.51	2.44	121	13.58	7.51	6.07
82	6.08	3.61	2.47	122	13.73	7.61	6.12
83	6.21	3.71	2.50	123	13.88	7.71	6.17
84	6.34	3.81	2.53	124	14.03	7.81	6.22
85	6.47	3.91	2.56	125	14.18	7.91	6.27
86	6.60	4.01	2.59	126	14.33	8.01	6.32
87	6.73	4.11	2.62	127	14.48	8.11	6.37
88	6.86	4.21	2.65	128	14.63	8.21	6.42
89	6.99	4.31	2.68	129	14.78	8.31	6.47
90	7.12	4.41	2.71	130	14.93	8.41	6.52
91	7.25	4.51	2.74	131	15.08	8.51	6.57
92	7.38	4.61	2.77	132	15.23	8.61	6.62
93	7.51	4.71	2.80	133	15.38	8.71	6.67
94	7.64	4.81	2.83	134	15.53	8.81	6.72
95	7.77	4.91	2.86	135	15.68	8.91	6.77
96	7.90	5.01	2.89	136	15.83	9.01	6.82
97	8.03	5.11	2.92	137	15.98	9.11	6.87

* for information only - do not enter on P11

Fig 6.4(a) (Crown copyright)

A   *6 April 1995 to 5 April 1996*

Weekly table for not contracted-out standard rate contributions

Earnings on which employee's contributions payable 1a	Total of employee's and employer's contributions payable 1b	Employee's contributions payable 1c	Employer's contributions*	Earnings on which employee's contributions payable 1a	Total of employee's and employer's contributions payable 1b	Employee's contributions payable 1c	Employer's contributions*
£	£	£	£	£	£	£	£
138	16.13	9.21	6.92	198	29.10	15.21	13.89
139	16.28	9.31	6.97	199	29.27	15.31	13.96
140	16.43	9.41	7.02	200	29.44	15.41	14.03
141	16.58	9.51	7.07	201	29.61	15.51	14.10
142	16.73	9.61	7.12	202	29.78	15.61	14.17
143	16.88	9.71	7.17	203	29.95	15.71	14.24
144	17.03	9.81	7.22	204	30.12	15.81	14.31
145	17.18	9.91	7.27	205	36.87	15.91	20.96
146	17.33	10.01	7.32	206	37.07	16.01	21.06
147	17.48	10.11	7.37	207	37.27	16.11	21.16
148	17.63	10.21	7.42	208	37.48	16.21	21.27
149	17.78	10.31	7.47	209	37.68	16.31	21.37
150	20.94	10.41	10.53	210	37.88	16.41	21.47
151	21.11	10.51	10.60	211	38.08	16.51	21.57
152	21.28	10.61	10.67	212	38.28	16.61	21.67
153	21.45	10.71	10.74	213	38.49	16.71	21.78
154	21.62	10.81	10.81	214	38.69	16.81	21.88
155	21.79	10.91	10.88	215	38.89	16.91	21.98
156	21.96	11.01	10.95	216	39.09	17.01	22.08
157	22.13	11.11	11.02	217	39.29	17.11	22.18
158	22.30	11.21	11.09	218	39.50	17.21	22.29
159	22.47	11.31	11.16	219	39.70	17.31	22.39
160	22.64	11.41	11.23	220	39.90	17.41	22.49
161	22.81	11.51	11.30	221	40.10	17.51	22.59
162	22.98	11.61	11.37	222	40.30	17.61	22.69
163	23.15	11.71	11.44	223	40.51	17.71	22.80
164	23.32	11.81	11.51	224	40.71	17.81	22.90
165	23.49	11.91	11.58	225	40.91	17.91	23.00
166	23.66	12.01	11.65	226	41.11	18.01	23.10
167	23.83	12.11	11.72	227	41.31	18.11	23.20
168	24.00	12.21	11.79	228	41.52	18.21	23.31
169	24.17	12.31	11.86	229	41.72	18.31	23.41
170	24.34	12.41	11.93	230	41.92	18.41	23.51
171	24.51	12.51	12.00	231	42.12	18.51	23.61
172	24.68	12.61	12.07	232	42.32	18.61	23.71
173	24.85	12.71	12.14	233	42.53	18.71	23.82
174	25.02	12.81	12.21	234	42.73	18.81	23.92
175	25.19	12.91	12.28	235	42.93	18.91	24.02
176	25.36	13.01	12.35	236	43.13	19.01	24.12
177	25.53	13.11	12.42	237	43.33	19.11	24.22
178	25.70	13.21	12.49	238	43.54	19.21	24.33
179	25.87	13.31	12.56	239	43.74	19.31	24.43
180	26.04	13.41	12.63	240	43.94	19.41	24.53
181	26.21	13.51	12.70	241	44.14	19.51	24.63
182	26.38	13.61	12.77	242	44.34	19.61	24.73
183	26.55	13.71	12.84	243	44.55	19.71	24.84
184	26.72	13.81	12.91	244	44.75	19.81	24.94
185	26.89	13.91	12.98	245	44.95	19.91	25.04
186	27.06	14.01	13.05	246	45.15	20.01	25.14
187	27.23	14.11	13.12	247	45.35	20.11	25.24
188	27.40	14.21	13.19	248	45.56	20.21	25.35
189	27.57	14.31	13.26	249	45.76	20.31	25.45
190	27.74	14.41	13.33	250	45.96	20.41	25.55
191	27.91	14.51	13.40	251	46.16	20.51	25.65
192	28.08	14.61	13.47	252	46.36	20.61	25.75
193	28.25	14.71	13.54	253	46.57	20.71	25.86
194	28.42	14.81	13.61	254	46.77	20.81	25.96
195	28.59	14.91	13.68	255	46.97	20.91	26.06
196	28.76	15.01	13.75	256	47.17	21.01	26.16
197	28.93	15.11	13.82	257	47.37	21.11	26.26

* for information only - do not enter on P11

Fig 6.4(b) (Crown copyright)

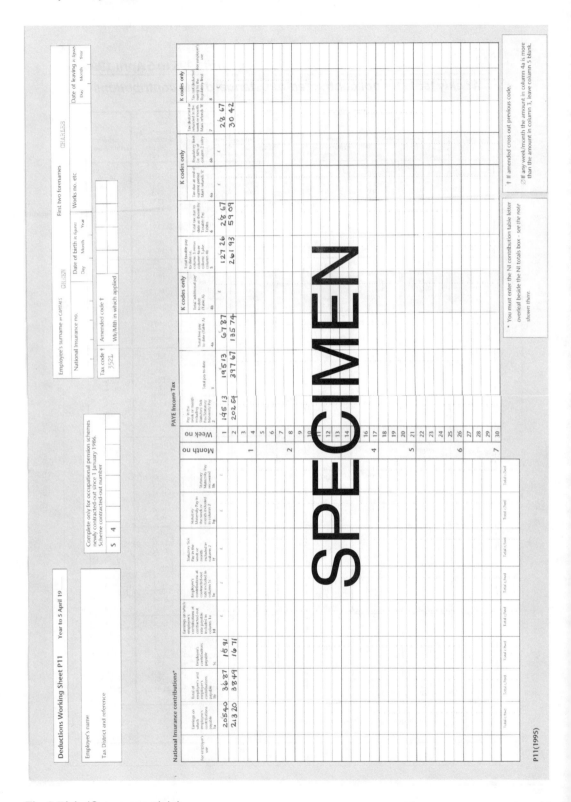

Fig 6.5(a) (Crown copyright)

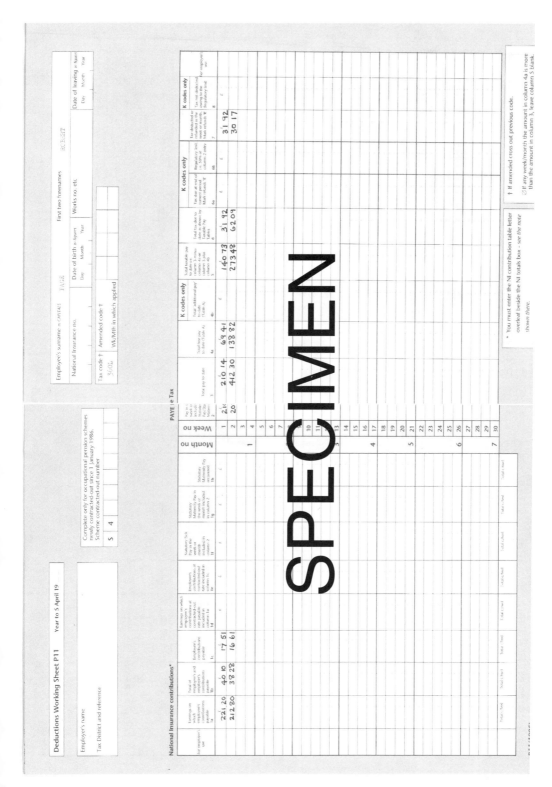

Fig 6.5(b) (Crown copyright)

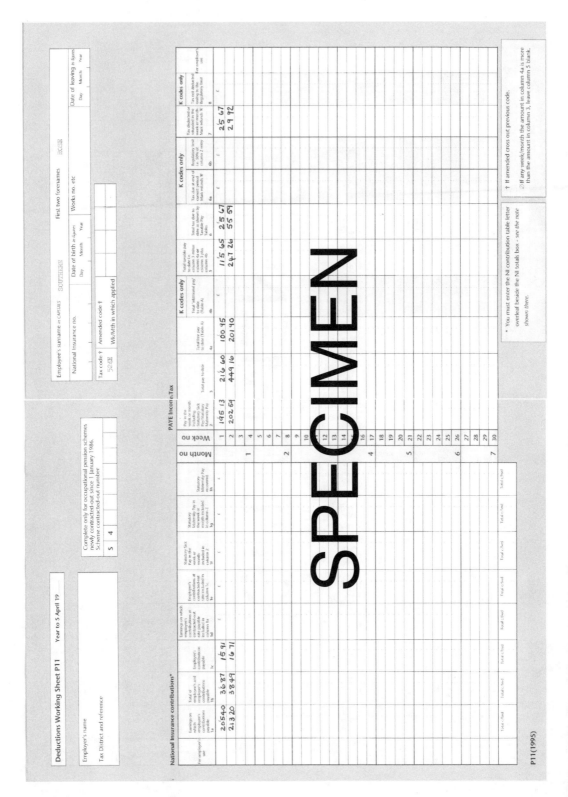

Fig 6.5(c) (Crown copyright)

Employee's surname *in CAPITALS*	TILLING		First two forenames		NAOMI	

schemes
'86.

National Insurance no.		Date of birth *in figures*			Works no. etc			Date of leaving *in*
		Day	Month	Year				Day	Month

Tax code †	Amended code †							Date of leaving
354L	Wk/Mth in which applied				

PAYE Income Tax

Week no	Pay in the week or month including Statutory Sick Pay/Statutory Maternity Pay 2	Total pay to date 3	Total free pay to date (Table A) 4a	**K codes only** Total 'additional pay' to date (Table A) 4b	Total taxable pay to date i.e. column 3 *minus* column 4a or column 3 *plus* column 4b 5	Total tax due to date as shown by Taxable Pay Tables 6	**K codes only** Tax due at end of current period Mark refunds 'R' 6a	Regulatory limit i.e. 50% of column 2 entry 6b	Tax deducted or refunded in the week or month. Mark refunds 'R' 7	**K codes only** Tax not deducted owing to the Regulatory limit 8	For em u
1	150 00	150 00	68 25	£	81 75	17 17	£	£	17 17	£	
2	150 00	300 00	136 50		163 50	34 59			17 42		
3											
4											
5											
6											
7											
8											
9											
10											
11											
12											
13											
14											
15											
16											
17											
18											
19											
20											
21											
22											
23											
24											
25											
26											
27											
28											
29											
30											

SPECIMEN

* You must enter the NI contribution table letter overleaf beside the NI totals box - *see the note shown there.*

† If amended cross out previous code.

∅ If any week/month the amount in column 4a is than the amount in column 3, leave column 5 b

Fig 6.6 (Crown copyright)

6

a Complete the time sheet in Fig 6.7 and calculate the gross wages. P Barber is paid £5.00 per hour for a 40 hour week and is paid time and a half for overtime.

b Explain:
  i free pay
  ii income tax code number
  iii statutory deductions
  iv National Insurance contributions
  v coin analysis
  vi tax tables

7 The net take-home pay for the week ending 27 January 19– (no 42) for the following employees of the Despatch and Warehouse Section has been calculated, but that for Richard Booth has not yet been completed:

John Foster	– £98.51
Barry Jones	– £103.60
Eric Palfreyman	– £88.96

a You have been asked to complete a copy of the payslip in Fig 6.8 using the following information:
  Richard Booth pays £1.25 per week to the Sports Club. His subscription to the Trade Union is paid by a £1.20 per week deduction.

b Make out a cash analysis sheet for the four employees.

c Complete a cheque to withdraw this money from the bank but do not sign the cheque.

8 The following are the net salaries of the data entry clerks at Systems Furniture plc:

	£
A Jackson	109.26
P R Richardson	120.42
R Southern	135.31
G A Lucas	92.54
N Aspinall	155.69

You are required to calculate the number of coins and notes required to pay the salaries of the five employees. You should not use notes of a greater denomination than £20 and issue each employee with at least five £1 coins.

9 P Griffith, A Johnson and S Lake, Sales Representatives of Systems Furniture plc, are paid a basic monthly salary but also earn a sales commission of 3½% if they secure sales in excess of £8000 per month. In March they each obtained the following orders:

	£
P Griffith	13 500
A Johnson	7 500
S Lake	10 000

Calculate the gross sales commission of each representative for the month of March.

10 You receive the following telephone calls from members of staff concerning their pay. Draft notes for your replies.

a Charles Vaughan:
  'I am leaving the firm next week to start another job. How will my new employer know how much tax to deduct?'

b Rose O'Brien:
  'The firm has agreed to let me work mornings only at half-pay. How will this affect the amount of income tax I pay?'

c Bob Inge:
  'I am off work with a broken arm and my Doctor says I will not be able to return to work for at least 3 weeks. What am I expected to do about my pay?'

► COMPUTER/WP TASKS

11

a Use a computer wages package to prepare (i) the pay advice slips for each of the employees in Tasks 1–3 and (ii) the payroll for Weeks 1–3.

b Your company wishes to pay all their employees monthly by credit transfer rather than by cash weekly. Use a word processor to prepare a draft standard letter to the employees asking them if they would agree to this proposal. After approval the letter will be merged with the employees' names and addresses to provide individual personalised letters.

c What are the advantages and disadvantages to the company and to the employees of using this method of payment for wages?

P Barber							NO 1234
Day	In	Out	In	Out	In	Out	Total
Monday	07.30	12.30	13.30	17.30			
Tuesday	07.30	12.30	13.30	17.30	18.00	20.30	
Wednesday	07.30	12.30	13.30	17.30			
Thursday	07.30	12.30	13.30	17.30	18.00	20.30	
Friday	07.30	12.30	13.30	17.30			
Saturday	09.00	12.30	13.30	17.00			
Sunday							

....................hours at.................. £........................

....................hours at.................. £........................

Total gross pay £........................

Fig 6.7

PAY ADVICE				
WEEK OR MONTH NO	DATE			
	DETAILS			
EARNINGS	A		–	–
	B		–	–
	C		–	–
	D		–	–
	E		–	–
	GROSS PAY		140	19
	PENSION/SUPERANNUATION		–	–
			–	–
	GROSS PAY FOR TAX PURPOSES		140	19
	GROSS PAY TO DATE FOR TAX PURPOSES		2955	55
	TAX FREE PAY		990	45
	TAXABLE PAY TO DATE		1965	10
	TAX DUE TO DATE		589	50
	TAX REFUND		–	–
DEDUCTIONS	TAX		24	45
	NI CONTRIBUTION		9	41
	0			
	1			
	2			
	3			
	4			
	5			
	6			
	TOTAL DEDUCTIONS			
NET PAY				
F			–	–
G			–	–
TOTAL AMOUNT PAYABLE				
EMPLOYER	NI CONTRIBUTION			
	H			
CONTRACTED OUT CONTRIBUTION INCLUDED IN TOTAL				

YOUR PAY IS
MADE UP AS
SHOWN ABOVE

BOOTH, R

Fig 6.8

▶ WORK EXPERIENCE TASKS

12 Work in the wages section:

- check clock cards and calculate gross pay
- calculate net pay and complete employees' pay records, P11s, pay roll and pay advice slips
- prepare coining analysis and cash summaries
- prepare a cheque for signature to withdraw money from the bank
- make up, check and issue wage packets

Assess your work in these tasks against the following NVQ performance criteria

Element 7.2   Prepare a variety of documents
(Level 2)

Performance criteria

a Instructions are understood.
b Completed documentation meets the requirements of the workplace.
c Layout, spelling, grammar and punctuation are consistent and in accordance with conventions and house style.
d Corrections, when appropriate, are unobtrusive.
e Security and confidentiality of information is maintained.
f Copies and originals are correctly collated and routed, as directed.
g Where work is not achievable within specified deadlines reasons are promptly and accurately reported.
h Work is achieved within agreed deadlines.

Unit 7
Filing

1 Copy Fig 7.1 and enter in it the type of filing equipment and classification methods you would recommend for each of the applications listed. The first item has been completed as an example of the information required.

2

a Prepare an internal telephone index for Systems Furniture plc, include all staff names and arrange them in alphabetical order. Add their positions in the firm.

b Compile an alternative index containing the same information but arranged with the staff names grouped within departments arranged alphabetically.

3 In this assignment you are employed by Systems Furniture plc to assist with filing in the buying department. The following items have to be filed:

Double glazing catalogue from Crittall Limited

Invoice no 6294 from Thorn Domestic Appliances Limited

Organisation	Application	Filing equipment	Classification method
R W Fothergill & Co	Correspondence with clients	Vertical filing cabinet	Alphabetical by name of client
Systems Furniture plc	Correspondence in export dept – with customers		
Systems Furniture plc	Floppy disks in secretarial typing centre		
Systems Furniture plc	Engineering drawings in production dept		
Systems Furniture plc	Staff record cards in personnel department		
Systems Furniture plc	Petty cash vouchers in cashier's section		
Systems Furniture plc	Stock record cards in stores section		
Westshire County Council	Applications for further education grants		
Compton Community Association	Secretary's correspondence		
Salter Snacks Ltd	Expenses claim forms		

Fig 7.1

Correspondence with Jack Spencer (Electrical) Limited

Correspondence with G R Webb & Sons

Invoice no 6273 from City Electrical Services Limited

Photocopying equipment catalogue from Guarantee Office Equipment Limited

Invoice no 6238 from Harris Electronics Limited

Correspondence with Selco Limited

Invoice no 6251 from P J Browning Limited

Carpets catalogue from Solent Carpet Company

Correspondence with Thomas & Brown (Sheetmetal) Limited

Copy the three charts in Fig 7.2 and enter the above documents into the relevant boxes.

4 You are now required to assist with filing in the sales department. Below is a list of customers' names and their file numbers. Draw a strip index chart with twelve strips and enter these customers in alphabetical order. Use block letters.

Name	File No
Barry O D	813
Delamore J	39
Air UK Ltd	545
Davies Bros	345
18–20's Fashions Ltd	98
Anglia Building Society	124
Blunt, Taylor & Sons	764
ABC Systems plc	802
Domestic Appliance Service Centre	634
Checkley P R	501
Bowyer Electronic Supplies plc	621
Burton Borough Council	75

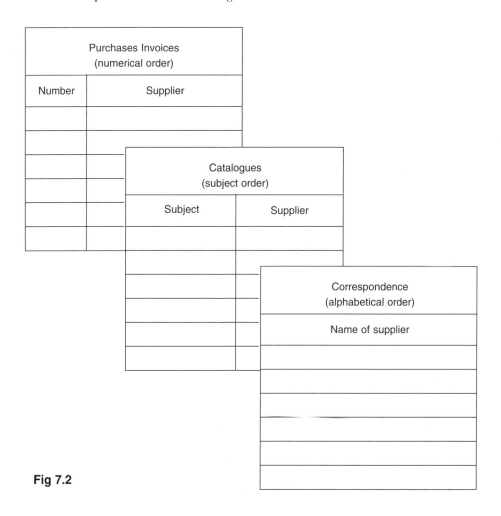

Fig 7.2

5 Your next work assignment at Systems Furniture plc takes you into the personnel department. Complete a personnel record card for a new full time employee, Miss Glenda Andrea Lucas (date of birth 21 May 1978) who lives at 14 River Park Road, Twyford, Westshire TD4 3BR. Telephone: 342186. Her next of kin is her mother Mrs Pauline Lucas who lives at the same address. Glenda has been engaged as a data entry clerk in the personnel department and she began work last Monday at a salary of £6200 per annum. The tax code stated on her P45 was 350L. She was previously employed by RIC (Engineering) Ltd.

6 You work in a firm called 'Frozen Fresh'.
a Sales are increasing and you are asked to rearrange customers' files into geographical order. Below are the names of customers in Essex:

Abbey Foods, Colchester	Fast Food Store, Colchester
Anchor Hotel, Chelmsford	The Freezer Store, Chalfont
Freezer Shop, Chelmsford	Healthy Foods, Colchester

Figure 7.3 illustrates the letter headings of some of the new customers in this area. Merge and put both sets of names onto a geographical index. Write the customers' names on the right hand side of each strip and the appropriate town on the left. Work from the foot of the index upwards, as these are the index strips on the top of the file pockets in a drawer.

Example:		
		Customer's name
	CHALFONT	Customer's name

b Explain why it will be beneficial to the sales representatives of your company for customers' names to be arranged in geographical order.
c Name one other type of firm which would find this to be an efficient method of classification.
d Frozen Fresh is sending a letter to all its customers, asking for an appointment on a set date. The letter has been prepared on a word processor, in preparation for the list of customers' names to be added. Describe the procedure for:
i   *storing* and *recalling* letters on a word processor
ii *safeguarding* them.
e Give three reasons why modern offices can operate more efficiently using electronic methods of storage.

7 You are about to go on holiday and you have been asked to leave clear instructions for the use of your filing system. You use a four-drawer vertical cabinet with linked suspension pockets. The top three drawers are arranged in alphabetical order of customers. The bottom drawer is arranged in subject order of other items you handle for your department.
a Provide specific guidance, in a point by point list, on the actual process you adopt to file papers.
b Provide two additional notes which will help maintain the accuracy of the system.
c Explain how you would add a new client file to this system.

(PQ OP1)

8 You had to cover the work of the filing clerk last week because she was off sick. You found this very difficult because many of the files were missing, sometimes information was filed in more than one file but there was no record of it, plans were piled up on top of the cupboards and some of the files were very bulky.

Prepare a report to the office manager, outlining the problems you found and suggesting ways in which:
a it would be possible to know if there were more than one file on a particular subject;
b it would be possible to trace the whereabouts of files at any time;
c plans can be filed without taking up too much space;
d papers are not kept any longer than necessary, but at the same time making sure that important papers are not destroyed.

(PQ OP2)

Fig 7.3

9 A common complaint in many organisations concerns the inefficiency of their filing system(s).
a Identify likely reasons for inefficiency.
b Make four suggestions which would help ensure increased efficiency and effectiveness, elaborating on each suggestion.

(PQ OP2)

10 There have been complaints to the Office Manager about the number of important documents which have gone astray recently. Four weeks ago you were asked to investigate the reasons for this situation and to recommend ways of improving the methods used for storing and retrieving documents.

During the course of your enquiries you discover the following:
a Managers take files out with them when they are visiting business associates.
b Some files, known by more than one name, cannot be found.
c Documents filed by subject classification are interpreted in different ways by filing staff, resulting in uncertainty and confusion when storing documents.
d The filing has grown with the company and each year more files are accumulated. Valuable office space is taken up by the cabinets and it is becoming increasingly difficult to find files, especially within the commonly-used alphabetic letters.

Write a report to the Office Manager outlining how you undertook your enquiries and making your recommendations for overcoming the problems.

(PQ OP2)

11 Some documents cannot be found in the filing system. Draft a report to the Office Manager in which you:

a identify four likely reasons for this failure;
b describe ways in which these problems can be avoided;
c recommend appropriate action.

(PQ OP2)

12 Make out index cards for the following:
a i   Mr John Edwards opened an account last Wednesday. His address is 27 Temple Street, Birmingham. He is moving to 28 Freeth Street, Walsall on the first of next month. His telephone number will be 01922 765211. His file number is 4001.
   ii   Yesterday Miss Lorraine Austin opened an account. Her file number is 4325. She is not on the telephone. Her address is 22 The Square, Wilmslow, Cheshire.
   iii   File No 4440 has been opened today for Mr Arthur West. His address is 65 Stanley Road, Wigton, Cumbria. His telephone number is 019654 334 865.
b Suggest two uses for these index cards.

(PQ OP1)

13 Referring to the Organisation Chart shown in Fig 7.4, suggest suitable filing equipment and classification systems for four of the five departments. Provide reasons to support your suggestions.

The Managing Director should not be included as his secretary deals with all his paperwork. You are expected to use suitable different classification systems.

(PQ OP2)

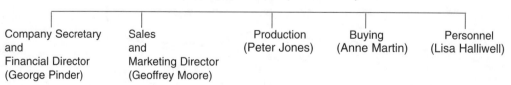

PINDER AND MOORE – ORGANISATION CHART
MANAGING DIRECTOR (Arthur Pinder)

| Company Secretary and Financial Director (George Pinder) | Sales and Marketing Director (Geoffrey Moore) | Production (Peter Jones) | Buying (Anne Martin) | Personnel (Lisa Halliwell) |

Fig 7.4

▶ **COMPUTER/WP TASKS**

14 A printout of a school database is shown below:

Surname	Forename	Form	Student no
Davis	Paul	5A2	500
Smithe	Angela	5B2	507
McDonald	Judy	5A3	508
Van Dam	Ruth	5B1	509
Farmerton	Peter	5A4	513
Smith	Paul	5B2	515
Farmer	Gladys	5A2	529
Davies	Derek	5A1	537
Vandenburg	David	5B3	539
MacDonald	Rosemary	5B2	551

i   Which filing calssification has been used?
ii Write out all the names again, this time arranging them in strict alphabetical order.
iii Give two reasons why you think the school has not used alphabetical order for its pupils.
iv Draw an absent card to be used in place of Gladys Farmer's file.

(PQ OP1)

15 In order to save space, Elizabeth Berger, Company Secretary and Financial Director of Universal Books Ltd, has suggested the possibility of transferring all of the firm's records to microfilm. You have been asked to investigate. Write a report to her drawing attention to:
a possible ways of changing documents to microfilm;
b the advantages and any disadvantages of microfilming;
c how safety and confidentiality could be ensured.

(PQ OP2)

16
a Using the data file prepared for Task 17 (Unit 2) and Task 15 (Unit 4), retrieve and make a note of the following data:
i   the address of R L Kennedy Ltd
ii the total value of the orders placed by Computerland plc in January and February

iii the amount owing by P W Moore & Sons at the end of February
b i Use a word processor to prepare the internal telephone index for Systems Furniture plc as required in Task 2 (a).
ii What advantages are gained by using a word processor for this task?

▶ **WORK EXPERIENCE TASKS**

17 Work in the central filing section:
● sort correspondence ready for filing
● file correspondence in existing files
● open new files, as required
● maintain records of file movements
● use microfilm equipment to locate and copy documents
● prepare index cards
● thin out files in accordance with a file retention policy
● use a VDU to retrieve data held on computer

Assess your work in these tasks against the following NVQ performance criteria

ELEMENT 6.1   Store information using an established storage system
(Level 1)

Performance criteria
a Information is stored promptly, in correct location and sequence.
b Stored materials are undamaged, safe and secure.
c Information is classified correctly.
d Classification queries are referred to the appropriate person.
e Systems for locating information are up to date, accurate and in a prescribed form.

ELEMENT 6.2   Obtain information from an established storage system
(Level 1)

Performance criteria
a Required information is promptly located, obtained and passed to correct person or location.
b Delays in the supply of information are notified and reasons for delay politely explained.
c Information obtained is correctly recorded, up to date and in the required form.
d Missing or overdue items are identified and correct procedures followed to locate them.

ELEMENT 5.1   Maintain an established storage system
(Level 2)

Performance criteria
a New information is put into the storage system following organisational procedures.
b Stored material is maintained in good condition in appropriate location.
c Item movements are monitored and recorded accurately.
d Overdue items are identified and systems for return implemented.
e Out of date information is dealt with as directed.
f Opportunities for improving established systems are identified and appropriate action taken.
g Work practices conform to organisational requirements.

ELEMENT 5.2   Supply information for a specific purpose
(Level 2)

Performance criteria
a Information requirements are understood.
b Information sources are correctly identified and accessed.
c Where available information does not match requirements, options and alternatives are identified and offered.
d Information is correctly transcribed and compiled.
e The information supplied is in an appropriate form.
f Essential information is supplied within required deadlines.
g Confidential information is disclosed only to authorised persons.

Unit 8
Incoming and outgoing mail

1 You are required to assist Sarah Bates with the opening and distribution of the incoming mail at R W Fothergill & Co.

a What action will you take with the mail received in the morning's post (Fig 8.1)?

b Mr Fothergill asks you to circulate a document received from the Health and Safety Executive to all partners. Prepare a circulation slip to accompany the document.

c Enter the following remittances received in the morning's mail in a remittances book:

	Amount	A/c no
Cheques:		
J R Francis	£45.26	51234
L M Watkins	£500.00	52178
Moreton & Sons	£39.50	51978
Postal order:		
R Johnson	£2.50	-
Cash:		
B Roberts	£15.00	51246
C Brown	£22.00	52123

2

a Using a current leaflet which shows the inland postal rates, calculate the necessary postage for each item which has to be despatched from your mailroom:

  i   letter weighing 148g – valued at £200 – by registered post

  ii letter weighing 295g to go second class

  iii urgent parcel weighing 3¼kg (next day delivery)

  iv letter weighing 80g – first class – recorded delivery

  v compensation fee parcel weighing 2¼kg valued at £80

  vi letter weighing 200g to go first class

b The above items of mail were received too late for inclusion in the department's mail and you are required to use postage stamps for

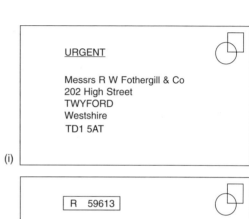

(i)

(ii)

(iii)

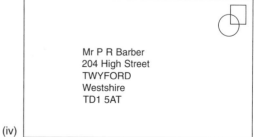

(iv)

Fig 8.1

them. Keep a record in a postage account of the total number of stamps used. The total value of stamps brought forward from the previous day was £30. Show the balance of stamps carried forward after stamping the mail.

3 In this assignment assume that you are employed with Glenda Attwood in the mailroom at Systems Furniture plc. Mail baskets are provided for each director and executive. Copy Fig 8.2; for each item state:
a which mail basket you would place it in;

b any additional action you would take before placing it in the basket (you can assume that all enclosures have been clipped to their relevant documents and that the post has been date stamped); the first item has been completed as an example.

4 Tony Miles was recently appointed sports secretary at Compton Community Association and up to now he has not recorded the postage stamps he has used in writing letters for the Association. During the course of a month he

Item	Mail basket	Additional action
a Cheque for £49.50 received from Westshire County Council	P T Watkins	Remittance checked and entered in remittances book
b Letter marked 'PRIVATE' addressed to the Managing Director		
c An order from a customer in Germany		
d A letter for the attention of **all** directors		
e A letter from a customer in Leeds without the indicated enclosure		
f A printer's proof of an advertisement in a trade journal		
g A prospectus from the Westshire College of Further Education		
h A quotation for supplying timber from West Coast Timber Supplies		
i A letter saying 'I enclose my application form for the post of data preparation clerk' but the form is not enclosed		
j The trade journal *Office Equipment and Methods*		
k A letter marked 'URGENT' addressed to the Personnel Manager		
l A vehicle registration document for a company car		

Fig 8.2

has to write several letters arranging sports fix-tures, booking pitches and coaches and gener-ally keeping in touch with members involved in the sporting activities. It is suggested that he should initially be given £10 and at the begin-ning of each month his balance in hand should be restored to £10. Write a letter to Tony sug-gesting and illustrating a method for recording the stamps he uses and explaining how to bal-ance the account at the end of each month.

5 The sequence for outgoing mail in any large office can well be shown in a flow diagram. Use the words below to complete the diagram in Fig 8.3.

mail bag	first class letters
weigh	wrap and secure
weigh if necessary	initial sorting
second class letters	frank
label	parcels

6

a Prepare a circulation list/slip for the Company Secretary of Systems Furniture plc to use when distributing information from the Board of Directors to all executives of the company.

b Mrs A Johnson, Sales Representative for Scotland, has been with the company for 25

years and it has been decided to present her with a carriage clock in recognition of her loyal service. You have been asked to wrap up and send the clock by post to Mrs Johnson, with a covering letter from the Managing Director. Explain what steps you will take to ensure that the clock arrives safely and in good condition.

7 You work in the mailing section of Westshire County Council's Education Department. What action would you take in each of the following circumstances?

a A courier delivers a parcel which is in a dam-aged condition.

b You discover that a package received in the morning post has some nasty grease marks on the cover.

c A remittance advice slip for £40 is received in the morning post without the remittance.

d A letter marked 'Urgent' and 'Confidential' is received for Mr Jones, Deputy County Education Officer, but he is on holiday and his Secretary is away from the office on sick leave.

8 You are assisting in the Mail Room of Twentieth Century Textiles Ltd whose organisa-tion chart is shown in Fig 8.4. You have to sort the following items:

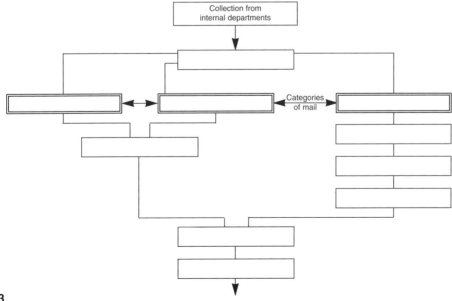

Fig 8.3

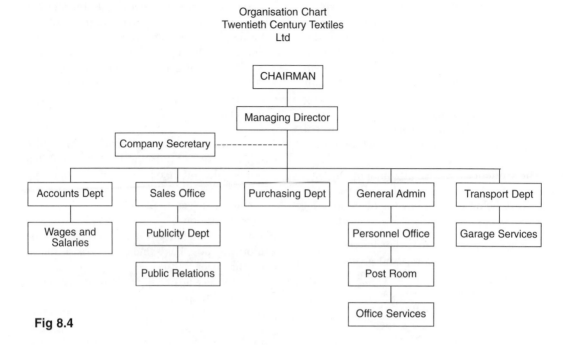

Organisation Chart
Twentieth Century Textiles
Ltd

Fig 8.4

a invoice for purchase of office furniture

b estimate for supply of dyes

c cheque for £1002.56

d a supply of blank P45 forms

e telephone bill

f a supplier's autumn catalogue and fabric samples

g draft copy from printers of the annual report and accounts

h application for secretarial post

i letter of complaint about a Twentieth Century dress fabric which was purchased by a lady in Leeds

j vehicle registration documents

By referring to the organisation chart, list the departments/sections which should deal with each item.

9 Mr K Pratt, the office manager of Systems Furniture plc, has asked you to let him know what advantages would be gained if he purchased an electronic franking machine and electronic scales. Supply this information to him in the form of a memo.

10 In this assignment assume that you are employed by R W Fothergill & Co. Mr P Green, the accountant, is considering the use of a franking machine for stamping outgoing mail and has asked you to supply him with the following information:

a Is a licence necessary?

b Does the post office supply the machine?

c Can a franking machine be used for parcels as well as letters? If so, how are they franked?

d Is it necessary to pay for the postage in advance?

e Do you have to keep a daily record of postage used?

f What happens if an error is made when franking an envelope? Is the postage wasted when this happens?

g Does the franked mail have to be prepared for posting in a special way? If so, explain how?

11 Your supervisor is reorganising the system of handling incoming mail and has asked you to:

a suggest four pieces of equipment that would be useful and briefly explain why they would be useful;

b suggest some things the mail clerk could do to help decide where to send documents that are only addressed to the company.

(PQ OP1)

12 You work in the mailing and communications centre.

a An A4 document has to be seen by all Heads of Department this afternoon. How would you deal with it?

b One Head of Department is in your other office 20 miles away. How would you ensure that she sees the document?

c A bulky brochure has been received which must be seen by three people. Prepare a circulation slip.

(PQ OP1)

▶ **COMPUTER/WP TASKS**

13

a Use a word processor to prepare the circulation list required in Task 6 (a) and print out a copy.

b Mr Watkins later asks you to add the Directors' names to the circulation list prepared in (a). Add these names to the Executives' names and print out a copy.

▶ **WORK EXPERIENCE TASKS**

14 Incoming/internal mail:

● receive and sign for registered and other special mail
● open, stamp, sort and distribute incoming/internal mail
● check remittances and enter them in a remittances book

Outgoing/internal mail:

● prepare outgoing mail for the post
● complete post office forms, as required
● deliver external mail to the post office and internal mail to departments

Assess your work in these tasks against the following NVQ performance criteria

ELEMENT 8.1   Receive, sort and distribute mail
(Level 1)

Performance criteria

a Procedures for receiving mail are in accordance with organisational requirements.

b Mail is sorted according to instructions within appropriate time scale.

c Mail is directed to the relevant person within appropriate time scale.

d Unavoidable delays in distribution are promptly reported to the appropriate person.

ELEMENT 8.2   Dispatch mail
(Level 1)

Performance criteria

a Procedures for dispatching mail are in accordance with organisational requirements.

b Any enclosures are securely attached and any missing items reported promptly.

c Mail is legibly and correctly addressed.

d Mail is dispatched within required deadlines.

ELEMENT 8.2   Receive and send mail
(Level 2)

Performance criteria

a Incoming mail is correctly processed and promptly directed to correct destination.

b Organisational procedures for dealing with suspect items are correctly followed.

c Outgoing mail is appropriately prepared for dispatch.

d The most appropriate mailing system, in relation to cost, urgency and security, is selected.

e Mail is dispatched within required deadlines.

Unit 9
Work planning and scheduling

1 In this assignment assume that you are working for Mr K Pratt, Office Manager of Systems Furniture plc.

a Enter the engagement given in Fig 9.1 in Mr Pratt's desk diary for Tuesday 4 April 19–.

b Reply to the card received from Business Technology Limited accepting their invitation to the office equipment exhibition.

c Look up train times from Bath (Mr Pratt's home town) to London for the visit to the theatre. He and Mrs Pratt will stay overnight in London. Select a four-star hotel and write a letter booking the necessary accommodation for the night. They will travel back to Bath by train the following morning and must be there no later than 1100. Prepare an itinerary for Mr Pratt's London visit.

2 You are working with Sarah Bates at the solicitors – R W Fothergill & Co. The Senior Partner has asked you to assist in making the arrangements for the firm's staff Christmas Dinner Party. A meeting has been arranged with Mr Fothergill in a week's time for you to discuss the matter. As a preparation for the meeting, draw up a checklist of the arrangements you will need to make for this event.

3 Tony Miles has been given the job of organising the next disco for the youth section of Compton Community Association. Compile a checklist of the action he will need to take to organise this event.

4 Design a weekly booking form for members of Compton Community Association who wish to use the Association's table tennis table.

5 Suggest two office tasks which the following are required to do in their jobs and against each task state (a) the planning required to perform it and (b) a diary entry associated with it:

   i   A Jackson, Assistant Secretary of Compton Community Association
   ii P Bell, Solicitor of R W Fothergill & Co
   iii C Bright, Advertising Manager of Systems Furniture plc
   iv P Buckingham, County Youth Officer responsible for the Youth Service at Westshire County Council
   v   Your supervisor at your place of work or at the firm where you gained work experience
   vi Yourself at your place of employment or where you gained work experience

6 In your office there are two dictating machines. When they were bought it was intended that one should be used by two executives for their dictation, and the other should be used by one typist-transcriber. However, sometimes both people want to dictate at once, and sometimes more than one transcriber works at the same time. This means that the two machines are frequently passed from person to person, and much irritation is caused because accessories, such as a foot control or a microphone, are missing. Search usually reveals that they have been put in somebody's desk drawer, and much time is wasted tracing the necessary parts before dictation or transcription can begin. It is proposed in future that you shall be responsible for the dictating equipment, and you are expected to devise a system whereby the borrower signs for what he or she takes. The equipment consists of two machines, four cassettes, two microphones, two headsets, two foot-controls and correction pads. List the rules you would make, and show how you would keep a chart or book, if you think one necessary.

The Directors of
Business Technology Limited
request the pleasure of the company of

Mr K Pratt

at the official opening of their

EXHIBITION OF NEW OFFICE EQUIPMENT AND AIDS TO EFFICIENCY

at the Twyford Showroom, 182 Caledonian Road

on

TUESDAY 4 APRIL 19—

at 1100

RSVP to C Adams, Branch Manager

*Booked!
for 4 April*

MESSAGE FOR

M ___ Mr K Pratt

WHILE YOU WERE OUT

M ___ Miss C Robinson
OF ___ Prima Office Machines Ltd
Telephone No ___ 0193-823194

Telephoned	✓	Please ring	
Called to see you		Will call again	
Wants to see you	✓	Urgent	

Message: Confirmed appointment to see you at 0930
on Tuesday 4 April 19—- to discuss the
typewriter maintenance contract.

Date ___ 2 April 19—-   Time ___ 1400
Received by ___ *J. Wilkinson*

Fig 9.1

7 A colleague of your employer celebrated their silver wedding anniversary in March. In February your employer asked to be reminded to write a letter of congratulation on the appropriate date. You have forgotten to do so. Your employer is extremely annoyed and, as this is not the first time such a situation has arisen, has asked you to devise a 'fool-proof' reminder system. What do you suggest?

8 The following ten people are all employed in one department: an office manager, a chief clerk (deputy office manager), the personal secretary to the office manager, two accounts clerks, two wp operators, a filing clerk, a telephonist and a mailroom clerk.

They are each entitled to a fortnight's holiday in either July or August. The filing clerk deputises for the telephonist, and one of the wp operators for the personal secretary. The other wp operator deputises for the filing clerk.

Make a holiday rota for the months of July and August.

9 You have been selected to attend a week's residential training course in another town to learn how to operate a new computer which is to be installed in your office.
a What information will you need to find out before you go on the course and what reference sources will you use?
b Describe six steps you will take to ensure that your work is covered properly while you are away, so that nothing will be overlooked.
c Give two methods by which you could be contacted urgently while you were away.

(PQ OP2)

10 Make a list of the daily activities which are done in your school/college office or the office in which you work and assess their priorities, ie jobs which *must* be done; jobs which *should* be done; and jobs which *could* be done.

11 In groups of two or three, you are required to plan an event. Your planning should include:
a a checklist;
b a time schedule;
c a plan of action indicating deadlines;
d memos, letters, programmes, invitation

cards, agendas, publicity leaflets, tickets, etc, required in the organisation of the event.
Suggestions for events:
a a fund-raising event;
b a school/college visit to a company/exhibition;
c a business trip abroad;
d an office party;
e an open day at your college or place of work;
f a conference.

12 If you do not obey the rules of courtesy when meeting people or when attending meetings, you may be labelled as arrogant, rude or a bore. Make a list of bad habits which might cause other people to regard you in this light and say what steps you should take to overcome these difficulties.

13 When you are choosing a career for yourself, which of the following factors will count most? List them in order of importance and give reasons for your choice.
a status;
b challenge;
c promotion opportunities;
d salary;
e 'perks' eg company car;
f job security;
g recognition for work done;
h sense of achievement;
i job satisfaction;
j responsibility;
k creativity;
l environment/working conditions;
m training opportunities.

14 Answer the questions given in the checklist on page 88 of *Office Procedures* about your personal performance at work or in work experience.

▶ **COMPUTER/WP TASKS**

15
a Use a computerised desk diary package to enter the staff holiday dates selected in Task 8 and print out a copy.
b Use a word processor to prepare a standard letter confirming telephoned hotel bookings

and use it to write to the London Hotel selected for Mr and Mrs Pratt in Task 1 (c).

▶ WORK EXPERIENCE TASKS

16 Work in the secretarial services unit:

- make appointments, confirm them by letter and record them in the office diary
- operate a follow-up system to bring forward matters requiring attention
- plan and organise booking procedures

Assess your work in these tasks against the following NVQ performance criteria

ELEMENT 1.1 Identify and agree own development needs
(Level 2)

Performance criteria

a Sufficient relevant information on own prior and current achievements is collected, to enable a valid assessment of development needs, to be made by self and relevant others.

b Opportunities for developing self are identified through matching own achievements against organisational needs.

c Identified needs for development relate to current work activities and potential career advancement.

d A formal statement of development needs is agreed with appropriate persons.

ELEMENT 1.2 Prepare and agree a plan of action to develop self
(Level 2)

Performance criteria

a Opportunities for meeting own development needs are identified and agreed with appropriate persons.

b Specific objectives for development of self are agreed with appropriate persons.

c Specific actions to facilitate development objectives are agreed with appropriate persons.

d Planned actions are documented in accordance with organisational procedures.

ELEMENT 1.3 Implement and review a personal development plan
(Level 2)

Performance criteria

a Actions are undertaken in accordance with agreed plan.

b Where planned actions cannot be met, alternative methods of achieving objectives are agreed with appropriate persons.

c Agreed objectives are reviewed with appropriate persons to determine achievement.

d An up to date record of progress against plan is maintained.

e A personal portfolio of achievements is established and maintained.

ELEMENT 3.1 Plan and organise own work schedule
(Level 2)

Performance criteria

a Routine and unexpected tasks are identified and prioritised according to organisational procedures.

b Appropriate planning aids are used to schedule work.

c Where priorities change, work schedules are adapted accordingly.

d Anticipated difficulties in meeting deadlines are promptly reported to the appropriate person.

e Assistance is sought, where necessary, to meet specific demands and deadlines.

ELEMENT 3.2 Obtain and organise information in support of own work activities
(Level 2)

Performance criteria

a Up-to-date information, relevant to own area of responsibility, is obtained and maintained.

b Information held is relevant and sufficient for work activities.

c Sources of information are regularly reviewed for usefulness and relevance.

d Information is organised into a suitable form to aid own work activities.

e Confidentiality of information is maintained in accordance with organisational procedures.

Section C
OFFICE TECHNOLOGY

• •

Unit 10
Computer systems and terminology

All practical tasks using computers and word processors are given in the units to which they relate.

1 Mr Pratt wishes to report to the Managing Director on possible new technology applications at Systems Furniture plc. He needs to identify unnecessary waste within the firm and to show where improvements could be made.

a In the form of a report, addressed to the Managing Director:

i   identify three areas of inefficiency in the present systems

ii   suggest how the introduction of computers and word processors would improve the system, indicating what kinds of software should be used

iii detail other items of equipment which should increase efficiency if introduced.

b Using graph paper, sketch a graphical method of presenting information about the anticipated savings. You should include a comparison with present support staff costs which break down as follows:

Keyboarding 34% Checking 5% Copying 3% Calculating 12% Filing 4% Telephone and meetings 18% Clerical and other duties 24%

Alternatively use a spreadsheet for the task

c Discuss three problems which may arise with the introduction of new technology into an existing work system.

2 Systems Furniture plc acquires some laptop computers. Suggest how they could make use of this equipment.

3 Computers are being used increasingly in offices. Give a list of office functions for which a computer can be used and outline the advantages of using a computer as compared with other methods.

4 Name three office procedures for which computers are now being used by some organisations. What are the advantages of using computers for these purposes and what factors should be considered before deciding to computerise any given procedure?

5 Pamela Sherwin, Secretary to Mr R W Fothergill, Senior Partner of R W Fothergill & Co, has recently had new, integrated word processing/spreadsheet/database packages installed on her computer.

How would you advise her to make use of the spreadsheet and database elements of the package?

6 Discuss the steps which you would expect each of the case study organisations to have taken to comply with the Data Protection Act 1984.

7 In your work as a temporary administrative assistant at the Westshire County Council's Education Office, you have access to computerised personal records of students. What steps would you expect to be in place to prevent unauthorised persons gaining access to these records?

8

a Outline the advantages which Systems Furniture plc, their employees and their customers will have gained from the use of computers and word processors.

b Are there any disadvantages which have resulted from the computerisation of office procedures and systems?

9 Word processors and disks require care in their operation and maintenance.

a Prepare a list of instructions for new staff on operating and caring for the machines.

b Give three handling precautions for disks.

(PQ OP1)

10 You have recently attended a word processing course. Your supervisor has asked you to provide a list of the features you would expect a new system to have with regard to the:

a hardware;

b software.

Give reasons for your choice.

(PQ OP1)

11 The Board of Directors are concerned that many of their office procedures are still being done manually. They wish to know the benefits of using a computerised system for stock control.

a Explain the advantages.

b List three possible health problems which computer operators might experience and explain how these could be avoided.

(PQ OP2)

Unit 11
Reprography

1 In order to raise funds for Compton Community Association it is proposed to hold a disco featuring the Twyford Twisters on Friday 7 May 19– at St Luke's Church Hall, Compton, from 2000 hrs to 0100 hrs. Each of the 120 members is to receive a separate invitation which admits two on payment of £12 at the door.

a Draw up a suitable layout for the invitation on A6 paper.

b Explain what equipment you will use to produce the invitation cards and to address the envelopes. Give your reasons for the processes selected.

2 Mr P Green, the accountant at R W Fothergill & Co, is considering how to address envelopes for the regular despatch of insurance premium renewal notices and asks you to supply the answers to the following questions:

a What different processes can be used for addressing labels and forms?

b How are the records prepared?

c How are the envelopes/labels produced?

d How are the records kept up to date when changes take place?

Type a memo to Mr Green supplying the answers to these questions.

3 Carol Pitman has recently acquired a small desktop copier for the secretarial work connected with Compton Community Association.

a What materials will she need in order to use this machine?

b For what community association purposes can the machine be used?

c What advice would you give Carol concerning the care and maintenance of the copier?

4 You are employed at Systems Furniture plc. Reply to Mr Bright's memo (Fig 11.1) which he left on your desk this morning.

5 If you were responsible for operating a copier, what action would you take to correct each of the following faults?

a the impressions on the copies are too faint to read

b the text on the copies has uneven margins

c the copy paper will not feed through the machine

d the printing on the reverse side of an original appears on the front side of the copies

e only part of an original will fit on to the copy paper

f the copier does not work

6 Your manager is considering buying a new copier for your department which consists of 12 staff, some of whom do a lot of copying in the course of a month.

a Provide a list of facilities which you think a new machine should have, giving reasons/explanations.

b Suggest a system by which the manager can identify the volume of copying done by each member of the department, explaining briefly how such a system would operate.

(PQ OP1)

7 You wish to produce 100 copies of the office newsletter. Choose the copying equipment with which you are familiar and describe:

a the basic principles of the process;

b the equipment and materials required;

c the preparation/processing of the material to be reproduced;

d mention any special advantages/disadvantages of using this system of copying.

(PQ OP1)

Memo

To   *Assistant*

From   *C. Bright*

Date   *1 March 19 -*

Subject

Our printing bills for advertising literature are 'sky' high and too near our budget limits for my liking.

Are there any ways in which we could do this work 'in house' but still retain the high standard of printing? I would welcome your advice.

Fig 11.1

8
a Prepare a checklist of tasks including the equipment necessary for the preparation and despatch of a circular letter of four pages to 500 customers. Begin with the preparation of the draft text and end with the despatch by post. Set this out under the headings: Task, Equipment, Justification for equipment.
b Suggest two alternative methods which may be used to address envelopes for the circulars prepared in (a).

(PQ OP2)

9 Your company is considering investing in new, more sophisticated reprographics equipment. Currently it has only very basic copying facilities and relies on a local printer for all specialist work.
a What would be the main factors you would consider when selecting any new equipment?
b Outline four advantages and four disadvantages of discontinuing outside printing support.

(PQ OP2)

10 Your company is planning a sales drive which will include a personalised mail shot to all customers drawing attention to the new products.
a Suggest the most appropriate way of producing a three-page letter. Justify your suggestions.
b Describe how your supportive literature might be prepared.
c Select the six items that would be helpful to the mailroom in sending off this mailshot.

(PQ OP2)

11 Your firm is considering buying a new copier.
Write a memo:
a listing the features which you think the new machine should have;
b describing two systems which the firm could use to record the amount of copying done by each department.

(PQ OP1)

12 The Board of Directors have decided to hold a reception at the Royal Hotel, West India

Dock, E14, to launch the publication of a new series of business studies textbooks. The reception will be held four weeks from today's date from 1200 to 1430 hours and a buffet lunch will be served. 200 guests are to be invited.

a Prepare for Thomas Berger's signature a letter inviting guests to attend and explaining the reason for the reception. Say that several of the authors will be there to answer any questions. Full details of the dates of publication, prices, discounts, etc will also be available. A buffet lunch will be served. If attendance is not possible, full details of the books will be sent upon request.

b Explain what equipment might be used to produce and mail personalised letters.

(PQ OP2)

13

a Prepare an information booklet about the organisation where you work or where you gained your work experience which could be handed to new employees during induction. You should make your booklet as attractive and clear as possible and include illustrations and diagrams where appropriate. The following should be included:

i   the name and type of organisation and whether it fits into the public or private sector

ii where it gets its finance from

iii the purpose of the organisation and a description of its activities

iv a list of safety rules or guidelines for employees

v   facilities and benefits provided for employees

vi guidelines on how employees should deal with members of the public and why this is important

vii guidelines on how to establish and maintain good business relationships with colleagues at work.

b Look up prices of materials and calculate the cost of producing the booklet in the following quantities;

i   100 copies

ii   500 copies

iii 2000 copies

c Explain the procedure and equipment you would use to produce the booklet.

▶ **COMPUTER/WP TASKS**

14

a The word processing operator in your firm has prepared a letter to be sent to all customers in the Essex area. The letter specifies the dates and times when the sales representative would like to pay a visit to each firm. Explain *in detail* the operations required to create the necessary files and the process undertaken to combine the relevant sets of information.

b Explain the benefit to the firm of using a computer to send out a letter of this type.

c The following is a list of equipment used in your offices. Describe the use of three of these items and give an actual example in each case.

collator   punch and binder
copier   long arm stapler
franking machine   decollator

d Not only is office equipment expensive, but companies cannot run efficiently if it breaks down. State three ways in which office personnel can look after equipment to make sure that it runs smoothly.

15 Elaine Brookes, the proprietor of the Brookes Office Services Agency, decided to extend her firm's range of activities by investing in some up-to-date specialised mailing and paper handling equipment. She acquired a desk-top collator, jogger, folding machine, burster, decollator and a plastic spiral binding machine.

Use a word processor or desktop publishing system to prepare a draft leaflet advertising these new services. Explain what additional help the agency can now provide for small companies and stress how important it is to use top quality, professionally produced paperwork to influence their customers.

▶ **WORK EXPERIENCE TASKS**

16 Work in the reprographics section:

● operate copiers
● undertake routine maintenance and cleaning of equipment
● maintain records of work completed

- control stocks of stationery and accessories
- collate and staple/bind documents
- operate collating, folding and bursting equipment

Assess your work in these tasks against the following NVQ performance criteria

ELEMENT 7.2   Produce copies using reprographic equipment
(Level 1)

Performance criteria
a Produced copies are of the required quantity and quality
b Materials wastage is kept to a minimum.
c Copies are collated as instructed.
d Document pages are neatly and securely fastened when required.
e Copies and original documents are distributed according to instructions.
f Difficulties in achieving targets are promptly reported and the reasons politely explained.
g Procedures for dealing with problems in operating equipment are followed correctly.
h Confidentiality of documents is maintained.

ELEMENT 3.1   Follow instructions and operate equipment
(Level 1)

Performance criteria
a Instructions are understood before operating equipment.
b Operating procedures and techniques follow operating instructions.
c Procedures for dealing with problems in operating equipment are followed correctly.

ELEMENT 3.2   Keep equipment in a clean and working condition
(Level 1)

Performance criteria
a Cleaning of equipment and replacement of consumable items follow instructions.
b Safeguards taken are appropriate to the cleaning or replacement activity.
c Discarded items are disposed of safely and appropriately.
d The equipment and nearby work area are left in a clean and tidy condition.
e Identified equipment faults and risks are promptly and accurately reported to the appropriate person.

ELEMENT 3.3   Obtain and maintain physical resources to carry out own work
(Level 2)

Performance criteria
a Resources obtained effectively meet requirements of own work.
b Resources are stored safely and securely and are located to provide easy and quick access.
c Resources are obtained in accordance with organisational procedures.
d Damaged or unwanted resource items are dealt with in accordance with organisational procedure.

Unit 12
Calculators

1 In this assignment assume that you are employed by Systems Furniture plc. Use a calculator to prepare an invoice to Westshire County Council for three systems desks (cat no AS2) ordered last Monday (order no 18763).

> Terms: Delivered Twyford
> Payment one month after delivery
> Trade discount 12½%

2 Use a calculator to calculate the total value of the stock of stationery held by R W Fothergill & Co on 1 January 19– as supplied in the stock list in Fig 3.

3 Mr R Williams, the export sales manager of Systems Furniture plc, has recently returned from a visit to Japan as part of an overseas sales campaign. He has asked you to refer to a current issue of a daily newspaper to check the foreign exchange rate for Japanese yen and, using a calculator, to let him know how much sterling he will receive for the 20 520 yen which he brought back to this country.

4 Use a calculator to calculate the gross wages of P R Richardson from the time card in Fig 12.1.

5 Using a calculator check the calculations in the invoice in Fig 12.2. If you discover any

TIME CARD					
No 121			Name: P R RICHARDSON		
Week ending: 14 April 19–			Week No 2		
Day	In	Out	In	Out	TOTAL HOURS
M	0801	1203	1301	1700	
Tu	0800	1202	1300	1701	
W	0757	1159	1302	1702	
Th	0756	1158	1300	1658	
F	0800	1202	1301	1657	
TOTAL					

Ordinary time............hrs @ £ 4.60
(up to 38 hours)
Overtime...................hrs @ £ 6.90

TOTAL GROSS WAGES

£

Fig 12.1

INVOICE

No 912

From: SYSTEMS FURNITURE plc
Brookfield Industrial Estate, Twyford, Westshire TD3 2BS

Tel: 0193 384192

Telex: 342689
Fax: 0193 219673

VAT Registration No: 3027560 21

Date: 14 July 19--

To: Westshire County Council
      Shire Hall
      Twyford
      Westshire TD1 6PL

Terms: Delivered Twyford
         Payment one month after delivery

Completion of Order No 1896   dated 1 July 19--

Quantity	Description	Cat No	Price each £	Cost £	VAT rate %	VAT amount £
2	Executive desks	AE2	360	660.00		
2	Fixed pedestal – 3 drawer	AP2	100	200.00 860.00		
	Less 12½% discount			107.50 752.50	17½	131.69
	Plus VAT			131.68 620.82		

Delivered on: 12.7.-
         by: own van

Fig 12.2

errors copy out the invoice and insert the correct figures.

6 Complete Mr Johns' expenses claim form in Fig 12.3, using a calculator to make the calculations and referring to the mileage chart in Fig 4.4 for the approved mileage figures. Mr Johns travelled by car from the Systems Furniture plc Head Office at Twyford. The mileage allowance is 18p per mile.

▶ **COMPUTER/WP TASKS**

7 Systems Furniture plc received an enquiry

dated 1 March 19– from Computerland plc (see Customer Records page xviii for details of this company) for supplying the following systems desks for delivery not later than 14 March 19–:
    20 of AS1
    6 of AS2
    8 of AE2
a The Production Manager has confirmed that this consignment could be ready for delivery by Twyford Carriers Ltd on 12 March 19–. Use the maths facility on your computer or a spreadsheet (if these are not provided, use a separate calculator) to calculate the cost of this consignment, taking into account trade

EMPLOYEE EXPENSES CLAIM

Name: P. A. JOHNS   Employee No. | 0 | 1 | 2 | 4 | Departmental Code: | 0 | 9 |

Bank Code: | 2 | 0 | 1 | 3 | 4 | 6 | Bank account No. | 3 | 4 | 6 | 8 | 8 | 1 | 2 | 7 |

Date 19–	Particulars	Car Mileage	Public Transport	Car Hire	Hotel accommodation	Meals	Sundries	Total	VAT Recoverable
Jan 3/5	Research Seminar at Oxford				115 00	52 90	3 00		25 01
" 14	Trade Exhibition at Birmingham					17 25	2 00		2 57
" 28	Meeting at S'hampton with customer					34 50			5 14
Total Mileage		Mileage Amount							
		TOTAL AMOUNT DUE							

These expenses have been wholly, exclusively and necessarily incurred on authorised business

Signed _____

Authorised   Date

Fig 12.3

discount, VAT, etc.

b Using the wp file prepared for the blank quotation form in Unit 2 (Task 17*a*), complete a quotation to Computerland plc for the above transaction and date it 3 March 19–. Request Computerland plc to telex or fax their order by 5 March 19– at the latest.

▶ WORK EXPERIENCE TASKS USING A CALCULATOR

8 Work in the accounts department:

● Operate a calculator to perform calculations and check the accuracy of business documents
● Apply checks to ensure accuracy of calculations
● Complete records, as required
● Deal appropriately with queries

Assess your work in these tasks against the following performance criteria

ELEMENT 5.3   Check and process routine numerical information
(Level 1)

Performance criteria
a Numerical information is checked accurately.
b Inconsistencies are promptly reported to the appropriate person.
c The recording and processing of checked, numerical information is carried out as instructed.

Unit 13
Health and Safety

1 The setting for these tasks is the Head Office of Systems Furniture plc. The information you require to complete the work is given in the following:

Fig 13.1   - The ground and first floor plans of the Head Office building

Page 153   - Accident report form

and in *Office Procedures*:

Fig 13.2   - Fire/Evacuation procedure

a At 1100 on Monday 9 January 19– Mrs Rosemary Mason was using the front staircase to deliver some papers to Mr Shearing and slipped, hurting her right arm and shoulder. She was badly shaken and in a distressed condition. You were also on the stairs at the time of the accident and you immediately contacted the qualified first aid officer and arranged for assistance for Mrs Mason. You also collected a first aid box in case it was needed. Mrs Mason was made a little more comfortable but it was felt that it would be wise for her to be taken to the Twyford General Hospital for examination and possibly an X-ray.

  i   Who is the qualified first aid officer and where did you locate her?

  ii Where was the first-aid box stored?

  iii Complete an accident report form for this incident. Mrs Mason's address and date of birth will be filled in by the Personnel Department.

b On the afternoon of 10 February 19– it was decided to hold a fire drill when everyone was required to vacate the building.

  i   Explain the escape routes using the nearest exits which each of the following should take to reach the fire assembly point:

     ● The Board of Directors meeting in the Board Room

     ● The Export Sales Manager

     ● The Transport Clerk

  ii Geraldine Allan was late arriving at the fire assembly point as she was in the middle of typing an urgent lengthy report on her word processor and had stayed to finish the paragraph she was working on. Mr Anderson, the Safety Officer, was most concerned about the time she had taken to vacate the building and that she had left her word processor switched on. When he reprimanded her she was very annoyed and said she resented the time taken to 'play at escaping from fires'. She had been told by Mrs Fisher, her supervisor, that she must finish the urgent report that day and now she had lost 20 minutes, she would have to work late and would not catch her usual train.

Was Mr Anderson right in expecting busy staff to take part in a fire drill?

What do you think of Geraldine Allan's attitude to it?

How do you think Mr Anderson should deal with this situation?

Discuss these questions in your group.

c On 14 March 19– you were working in the sales office when an electric fan heater jammed and overheated, setting off a mass of sparks which fell on a pile of sheets of computer printout causing them to catch fire.

What action should you have taken? In your answer explain where the nearest fire extinguisher was kept.

d From 3-14 April 19– Gail Talbot, a student from Twyford Comprehensive School, will be working at Systems Furniture plc to gain office experience. You have been asked to show her round the offices and factory and

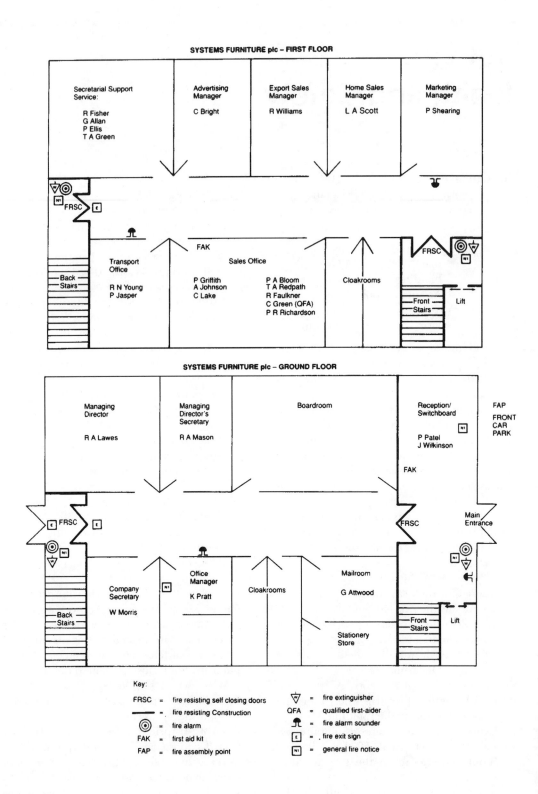

SYSTEMS FURNITURE plc – FIRST FLOOR

| Secretarial Support Service: R Fisher, G Allan, P Ellis, T A Green | Advertising Manager C Bright | Export Sales Manager R Williams | Home Sales Manager L A Scott | Marketing Manager P Shearing |

FRSC

Transport Office — R N Young, P Jasper

FAK

Sales Office — P Griffith, A Johnson, C Lake / P A Bloom, T A Redpath, R Faulkner, C Green (QFA), P R Richardson

Cloakrooms

FRSC

Back Stairs

Front Stairs — Lift

SYSTEMS FURNITURE plc – GROUND FLOOR

| Managing Director R A Lawes | Managing Director's Secretary R A Mason | Boardroom | Reception/Switchboard P Patel, J Wilkinson | FAP FRONT CAR PARK |

FAK

FRSC

Main Entrance

Company Secretary — W Morris

Office Manager — K Pratt

Cloakrooms

Mailroom — G Attwood

Stationery Store

Back Stairs

Front Stairs — Lift

Key:

FRSC	=	fire resisting self closing doors
—	=	fire resisting Construction
⊚	=	fire alarm
FAK	=	first aid kit
FAP	=	fire assembly point

▽	=	fire extinguisher
QFA	=	qualified first-aider
🜊	=	fire alarm sounder
E	=	fire exit sign
N1	=	general fire notice

Fig 13.1

to explain to her the firm's rules for health and safety. What would you tell her about the evacuation procedure for a fire or other emergency? Prepare the notes you would make for this aspect of your talk. Who and what would you point out concerning safety when you showed her round the building?

2 Miss R Fergus, Partner of R W Fothergill & Co, has been asked to take charge of health and safety for the firm.
a Draft a memo which she can send to all staff reminding them of their obligations under HASWA and pointing out some realistic examples of potential hazards in offices.
b Supply Miss Fergus with a note of the firm's obligations under HASWA.

3 You witness an accident which happened to Paul Grant of 14 Pine Road, Twyford (DOB: 14.11.78) at about 1030 on Thursday 4 May 19– while working in the Education Office at Westshire County Council. He was using a guillotine to cut up some cards when the guard fell away to expose Paul's hand to the blade. His right thumb was cut deeply causing heavy bleeding. Joan Baker, the first aid officer for the department was brought in quickly and she applied a sterile dressing and bandage. An ambulance was called and Paul was taken to the Twyford General Hospital where he received treatment in the Casualty Department.
a Complete an accident report form for the safety officer.
b What further action should be taken?

4 There is a fire extinguisher in the main hall of the Community Association, but there are no instructions on what to do in the event of a fire.
a Devise a suitable notice to be placed by the fire extinguisher explaining what action should be taken if there is a fire.
b What advice should be given to members of Compton Community Association about fire prevention in the hall?

5
a There have recently been several accidents caused by employees' carelessness and you have been asked to draft a memo to all staff pointing out the precautions to be taken in

the office under the following headings:
1 electrical equipment
2 carrying heavy items
3 storing and safe keeping of inflammable materials
4 floors and stairs
b Complete an accident report form using the details given in the accident statement made by Jayne Smith in Fig 13.2.

6
a Write a reply to the memo in Fig 13.3. Use the memo correctly to write your reply.
b State briefly two hazards which may occur when using each of the following:
i   filing cabinets
ii waste paper baskets
iii computers
c State the meaning of the following hazard signs:

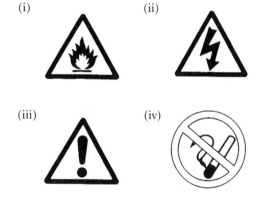

(i)   (ii)

(iii) (iv)

7
a The work station shown in Fig 13.4 belongs to the office junior who is on sick leave, having scalded a leg by tripping over a trailing flex while carrying a boiling kettle. The equipment on the junior's desk does not work properly, and the text on the floppy disk has been lost. Write a short report for the Office Manager listing eight points with regard to office safety and the use and care of office equipment that have been ignored. Indicate briefly why each point should be observed.
b List three steps you would take if any electrical equipment breaks down while you are using it.

```
┌─────────────────────────────────────────────────────────────────────┐
│  STATEMENT OF ACCIDENT GIVEN BY MISS JAYNE SMITH, RECEPTIONIST,       │
│  TO MR I JOHNSON                                                      │
│                                                                       │
│  2 February 199-                                                      │
│                                                                       │
│  Miss Patricia Morrison, Sales Department Clerk, had filled a         │
│  cardboard box with file folders which were to be taken down to       │
│  the basement.                                                        │
│                                                                       │
│  At approximately 9.30 am,. Peter Whorton, Management Trainee in      │
│  the Drawing Office, volunteered to carry the box downstairs          │
│  because he was returning a bottle of cleaning fluid to the           │
│  maintenance man. He balanced the bottle on top of the files and      │
│  proceeded downstairs to the basement.                                │
│                                                                       │
│  Peter had got to the middle of the stairs near the Reception         │
│  Area when he tripped over a parcel which I had placed there          │
│  temporarily.                                                         │
│                                                                       │
│  Peter sustained a twisted ankle and nasty cuts to his face and       │
│  right hand through falling on the broken bottle of cleaning          │
│  fluid. I rendered first aid and an ambulance took Peter to           │
│  hospital, but he was allowed home after treatment. He will be        │
│  away from work for at least five days.                               │
│                                                                       │
│  Peter's date of birth is 12 August 1974, and his home address       │
│  is 22 Millington Way, Lichfield, Staffs, SF2 1JL.                    │
│                                                                       │
└─────────────────────────────────────────────────────────────────────┘
```

Fig 13.2

8 You are working as a clerical assistant and are returning from lunch today with Lesley Grant who is wages clerk in the Accounts Department and Alan Thomas, administrative assistant in the Sales Department. You hurry through the company car park as you are due back at 2 pm and have only five minutes to reach your desks. Lesley trips on some uneven ground created by builders who are extending the offices.

The firm's nurse inspects the injury and, as she suspects a broken arm, Lesley is taken to hospital.

a Complete an accident report form. The date of birth and home address will be inserted by the Staffing section.

You consider that the state of the car park is dangerous. You saw a customer trip in the same spot yesterday.

b Write a short memo (two or three lines) to the Health and Safety Officer expressing your concern about the car park.

(PQ OP1)

9 There have been a number of minor accidents in your office recently. You have been asked by the Office Manager to:

a draft a memorandum from her to all the staff drawing their attention to the importance of safe working habits;

b refer specifically to two common causes of accidents.

You should prepare your draft and conclude your memorandum with a five-point list of recommended positive steps which staff can follow in the interests of safety.

(PQ OP1)

10 Before staff begin to use the new computers, they decide to hold a meeting because they are worried about the health and safety aspects.

To prepare for the meeting, make a list of possible points which staff may raise under the following headings: the screen, the printer, the work station and general working conditions. Suggest what preventative measures could be taken for each of the points raised.

(PQ OP2)

11 Sally Jones, a filing clerk in the Accounts Department, tripped on a broken entrance step at 8.30 am on her way into the building. It was raining heavily at the time. Mr Drake from the

TO
    Clerical Officer
    General Office
    (High Street Branch)

FROM
    General Office Manager
    Head Office

SUBJECT   Office Safety

MESSAGE   **DATE** 17 June 19--

During a recent visit to the General Office at your Branch, I was very concerned to note the following:

1. A jumble of electric cables around the reprographic machines, all coming from one socket and trailing across the walkway.

2. A junior filing clerk had climbed on a pile of telephone directories on a chair to reach some Lever Arch files placed on a top shelf.

3. When a clerk cut her hand the first aid kit from the Personnel Manager's car had to be used and I did not see this accident reported.

These matters must be dealt with immediately. Please inform me of the action taken.

SIGNED   *H. R Lewis*

REPLY   **DATE**

SIGNED

Fig 13.3

```
┌──────────────────────────────────────────────────┐
│ ┌─────────────────────────────────────────────┐  │
│ │                                             │  │
│ │              RECORD CARD                     │  │
│ │              ‾‾‾‾‾‾‾‾‾‾‾                     │  │
│ │                                             │  │
│ │   Sally Jones                               │  │
│ │                                             │  │
│ │   12 Park Road                              │  │
│ │                                             │  │
│ │   Wellington                                │  │
│ │                                             │  │
│ │   Tel No: _____  │  │
│ │                                             │  │
│ └─────────────────────────────────────────────┘  │
└──────────────────────────────────────────────────┘
```

Personnel Department was also climbing the steps and together you helped Sally Jones into the building. The company nurse was called. She bandaged Sally's ankle which was twisted and asked you to get a taxi to take her home. You looked up Sally Jones' address on the index cards when you ordered the taxi.

a Using the information supplied complete an accident form.

b Write a brief memorandum to the Health and Safety Officer enclosing the accident report form and requesting that steps be taken to prevent further accidents.

(PQ OP1)

12 As the company moves towards office automation, Anna Woods, Personnel Manager, is concerned about health and safety conditions in the office.

a Explain (with reasons) five ways in which management should provide for the health, welfare and safety of the office staff.

b On behalf of Anna Woods, prepare a draft notice stating that there will be a fire drill some time during the next week but do not give the date. Remind staff of the action to be taken in case of fire, listing at least six rules to be followed for safe evacuation from the building.

(PQ OP2)

13 The safety record of your company has deteriorated with a resultant increase in absence.

a The Personnel Manager asks you to draft a memo reminding employees of their responsibilities in respect of safety.

b Describe four actions that can be taken to improve safety in the office, indicating what types of accident would be prevented.

c Describe five ways of avoiding the problems associated with working with VDUs.

(PQ OP2)

► COMPUTER/WP TASKS

11 A new office project is in the planning stages at Systems Furniture plc to re-house eight of the accounts clerical staff. They will each have the use of a VDU on their desks. Four of the staff will be using computer facilities for the first time and they have expressed some anxiety concerning the effect which the VDUs might have on their health.

a What would you say to the staff concerning health problems associated with the use of VDUs?

b What steps should the office manager take in planning this new room to provide for the health and safety of staff? Draft your suggestions on a word processor and print out a copy.

► WORK EXPERIENCE TASKS

12 At the workplace:

● put into practice the safe-working rules given on pages 119–121 of *Office Procedures*.

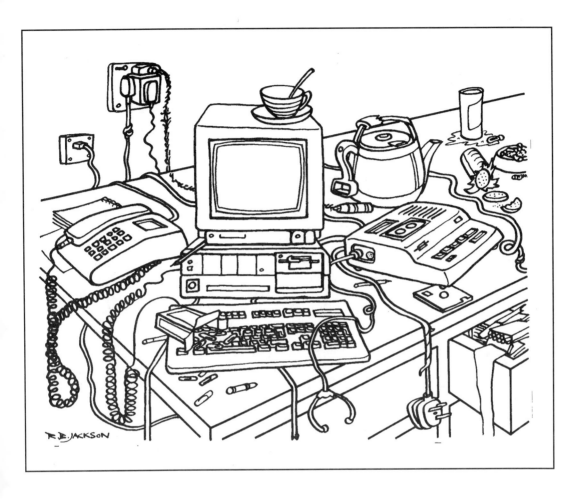

Fig 13.4

Assess your work in these tasks against the following NVQ performance criteria

ELEMENT 2.1   Monitor and maintain health and safety within the workplace
(Level 2)

Performance criteria

a Existing or potential hazards are put right if authorised.

b Hazards outside own authority to put right are promptly and accurately reported to the appropriate person.

c Actions taken in dealing with emergencies conform to organisational requirements.

d Emergencies are reported and recorded accurately, completely and legibly in accordance with established procedures.

e Work practices are in accordance with organisational requirements.

f Working conditions which do not conform to organisational requirements are promptly and accurately reported to the appropriate person.

g Organising of work area minimises risk to self and others.

Section D
COMMUNICATIONS

• •

Unit 14
Oral communication

1 Prepare notes and give a short talk to members of your group on one of the following topics:

a Opportunities for communicating orally in your job.

b Opportunities for communicating orally in the role of Sarah Bates, Amanda Jackson or Paul Grant.

c How to speak with 'a smile in your voice' when using the telephone.

d How to 'expand your market without leaving the office' with modern telephone services and facilities.

e How to 'win through an interview' by influencing the interviewer with your command of oral communication.

If possible, make a tape recording or video recording of these talks, so that you can judge your performance and see where improvements can be made on future occasions.

2 Sarah Bates has a new receptionist/telephonist (Marilyn Brown) working with her at R W Fothergill & Co on one month's trial. After the first week Marilyn, in a distressed and agitated state, asks to see Sarah privately. She explains that the job is getting her down and she is having sleepless nights worrying about it. Marilyn had been told off several times for the way she has spoken to visitors and to people on the telephone. She has found it embarrassing when she has had to meet visitors and sometimes explain that the partners they wanted to see are not available and she has had difficulty in convincing them that others were able to sat-

isfy their needs. Telephone callers have been irate, complaining that she is too slow and unhelpful when dealing with their calls. Marilyn is anxious to keep the job and has pleaded with Sarah to help her to improve her performance.

In pairs:

a role play Marilyn's conversation with Sarah and Sarah's advice to her;

b demonstrate, with appropriate examples, the techniques which Marilyn should be using to impress the visitors and telephone callers at Fothergill's.

3 Use a tape recorder to:

a record a telephone answering machine announcement for use at Systems Furniture plc in the evenings and at weekends when the offices are closed.

b leave a message on a telephone answering machine at Twyford Secretarial Services Ltd asking them to send a mechanic to Systems Furniture plc as soon as possible to repair a fault in the Xerox 1050 Copier in the Print Room. The mechanic should ask for Mrs R Fisher.

4 Sarah Bates, Amanda Jackson and Paul Grant are Compton Community Association's team for a public speaking contest to be held at the County Hall next month. They can choose a discussion topic of their own choice. What topic would you suggest? What advice would you give them and how should they prepare for the contest?

5 Discuss in your class the impact of new technology on office communications and the effects of a 'paperless office' on office workers.

6 Mr K Pratt, the office manager of Systems Furniture plc, is concerned about the high cost of telephone calls and he has asked you to design an eye catching diagram which could be displayed on noticeboards drawing the attention of staff to different ways of reducing telephone costs.

7 Using your local telephone directory, yellow pages, a fax directory and a telex directory compile the list of numbers in Fig 14.1 for quick reference by your telephone.

8 As you enter your office this morning, Polly, a girl in her first secretarial job, in the Advertising Department, is waiting for you in tears and is clearly very upset. She explains she is afraid to face her manager this morning because of a number of incidents yesterday afternoon. She had returned twenty minutes late from lunch only to find her manager at her desk, talking on the telephone, searching through a mass of mail and papers spread over her desk, and a visitor impatiently waiting in his office. In angry tones her manager was telling the caller he was certain a contract was sent to him two days ago, although he can't find the copy. Polly now admits to you that she had forgotten to enter the visitor in the diary because she left work early the previous evening, and on the way to work today discovered the contract, which should have been posted two days ago, in the bottom of her shopping bag. You now have to advise her *urgently*:

a how to cope with the problem of facing her manager and starting work *on time* today;

b what action she should take to avoid any repetition of similar incidents in the future.

Discuss in class the advice Polly should be given.

Organisation	Telephone No	Fax No (where applicable)	Telex (where applicable)	
			No	Answerback code
a three of your largest employers i ii iii				
b county council				
c district council				
d customs and excise				
e inland revenue				
f electricity company				
g college of further education				
h newspaper				
i office equipment supplier				
j chamber of commerce				
k accountant				
l solicitor				

Fig 14.1

9 Your company wishes to give every new employee some guidance on the efficient use of the telephone. They want you to provide suggestions for using the telephone efficiently and projecting a good image of the company.

Draft a notice listing guidelines for making telephone calls. Include suggestions for economy and efficiency.

(PQ OP1)

10 You work at Salter Snacks (*see* case study scenario). You are just going to lunch when you receive a telephone call from John Smith of Orpington Social Club. The latest batch of packets of salted cashew nuts are not of the usual quality. The outer boxes appear to have had something spilled on them, and he says that there were similar problems with the last batch. He would like Sarah to ring back as soon as possible (after 1600 hours as he will be out of the office until then). Sarah is in a meeting but will be back shortly. Fill in a message form.

(PQ OP2)

11 Describe the following services and in each case name a situation in which it would be used.
a Telephone conference call.
b Transferred charge call or collect call.
c Emergency service.

(PQ OP1)

12 You are asked to answer Jane Sheridan's telephone while she is at an important management meeting. Christine Dewar of Tiny Tots Clothes Ltd telephones her at 1415 hours about the non-delivery of an order for 80 T-shirts in assorted colours, size 2–3 years, which were promised by today's date. She says it is urgent that she speaks to Jane Sheridan as soon as possible. She can be contacted on 0171-653 9217.
a Complete a message form.
   While you were out of the office, Christine Dewar called again and left a message on the telephone answering machine. She asked if you would ring back and let her know if the following items are available from stock:

50 sweaters, Style 1578, size 4–5 years
60 pairs of jeans, Style 2246, in the same size and she is also interested in another 20 of the T-shirts referred to in her previous call.
Would you also confirm that the catalogue prices and terms are still applicable.

On checking, you find that all of the goods are available from stock at the quoted prices and terms. Delivery could be made within a week.
b Make the notes you will use when supplying this information to Christine Dewar.

(PQ OP2)

▶ COMPUTER/WP TASKS

13 Westshire County Council arranges for parties of students from local schools and colleges to visit the Shire Hall to see its office facilities and hear about the services provided by the Council for the public. The itinerary for the next tour includes a visit to the Education Department to see the computers in use.
Role play your talk to the students and be prepared to answer the following questions:
   i   How many letters can you store on a floppy disk?
   ii Apart from amending text, what else will a word processing package do?
   iii How does this equipment differ from the microcomputer that I have at home?
   iv Is it harmful to your eyesight to work for long periods on a VDU?

▶ WORK EXPERIENCE TASKS

14 Work in the marketing department:

● receive and give messages:
   face-to-face
   on the telephone
   on the telephone answering machine
● use the telephone to make and receive calls and, if required, transfer callers to others in the organisation

Assess your work in these tasks against the following NVQ performance criteria

ELEMENT 5.1   Process incoming and outgoing telecommunications
(Level 1)

Performance criteria

a Communications are responded to promptly and clearly using approved organisation manner.

b Callers are correctly identified and requirements established accurately.

c Queries are answered within own area of authority or referred to the appropriate person.

d Outgoing calls, for self or on behalf of others, are correctly obtained.

e Relevant information is courteously obtained and checked.

f Relevant information is communicated promptly and accurately to the appropriate person.

g Faults are promptly reported to the appropriate person.

h Recording of communications, when required, is in accordance with organisational procedures.

ELEMENT 5.2   Supply information to meet specified requests
(Level 1)

Performance criteria

a Relevant sources of information are correctly identified.

b Appropriate information is obtained and collated.

c Information is supplied to the appropriate person within required deadlines.

d Information is supplied in a form appropriate to the urgency and requirement of the request.

e Help is sought from the appropriate person when difficulties occur in obtaining information.

f Difficulties in achieving targets are promptly reported and politely explained.

ELEMENT 8.1   Receive and transmit information electronically
(Level 2)

Performance criteria

a The most appropriate transmission system, in relation to urgency, cost and security, is selected.

b The equipment selected is correctly used as laid down in operating instructions.

c Material is prepared accurately and correctly for transmission.

d Information is transmitted to correct location within required deadlines.

e Outgoing and incoming communications are dealt with in accordance with approved organisational procedures.

f Incoming information is promptly routed to correct location.

g Security and confidentiality procedures conform to organisational requirements.

h Any faults are promptly rectified or reported.

Unit 15
Written communication

1 You are employed in the marketing department of Systems Furniture plc and are required to deal with the letter in Fig 15.1 which was received from Micro Systems plc.

a Compose and type a reply from Mr L A Scott, the home sales manager, enclosing a copy of the catalogue and price list and say that Mr

Johnson has been asked to call on them some time during the next week. Tell them that several items of our furniture are being exhibited at the Business Efficiency Exhibition which will be held on 1 and 2 June 19– at the Empress Hall, Hull and invite them to visit our stand. Enclose two compli-

---

MICRO SYSTEMS plc
PO Box 133, 122 Baker Street, Hull HU3 7HR
Telephone: 01482 23519   Telex: 898237   Fax: 01482 61823

28 May 19–

Your Ref:
Our Ref: RJ/SH

Systems Furniture plc
Brookfield Industrial Estate
Twyford
Westshire TD3 2BS

Dear Sirs

Some months ago we received a call from your Representative
Mr A Johnson and he supplied us with a leaflet on your range
of office furniture. We will shortly be moving into new
larger premises and we will require additional office desks
and chairs.

Will you please arrange for us to receive your latest
catalogue and price list and we would also like Mr Johnson to
call to discuss our requirements.

Yours faithfully

R Jones

R. Jones
Office Manager

Registered in England No 1983479
Registered office as above

Fig 15.1

mentary tickets for the exhibition.

b Type a memo to Mr Johnson from Mr Scott enclosing copies of Mr Jones' letter and your reply in (*a*) above. Ask Mr Johnson to call at Micro Systems plc as soon as possible and to telephone Mr Scott when he has visited them.

c At 1430 on 6 June 19– Mr Johnson telephones from his home telephone 01482 251621. Mr Scott is engaged in a meeting and you receive the telephone call. Mr Johnson visited Micro Systems plc this morning. They will consider placing an order for ten systems desks if we can supply them with a width of 900mm (not in our normal range) and the normal 750mm deep and 680mm high. They will also require three drawer fixed pedestals for each desk. Please ask Mr Scott to send them a quotation and if possible allow them a generous trade discount. They would require delivery by the first week in July. Write out this message for Mr Scott on a telephone message sheet.

d Prepare the quotation requested in (*c*) to Micro Systems plc. The systems desks and pedestals can be supplied at the sizes requested for £380 each – offer valid for two months and terms to be as follows:

Net cash: one month
Price includes delivery costs but excludes VAT
Trade discount: 12½%
Delivery: 3 weeks on receipt of order

e Type a memo to Mr Johnson from Mr Scott and send a copy of the quotation prepared in (*d*). Suggest that Mr Johnson follows up this quotation in a week's time.

2

a Write a letter of application in reply to the advertisement in Fig 15.2 in the *Twyford Herald* for the post of secretarial assistant at R W Fothergill & Co.

b You receive a letter from R W Fothergill & Co inviting you to attend for interview at 1030 hrs on Friday 7 July 19–. Write a letter confirming that you will attend the interview.

3

a Write a letter for Carol Pitman in her capac-

SECRETARIAL ASSISTANT

required for firm of solicitors. Good text processing qualifications essential. Varied clerical duties. Usual paid holidays. Contributory pension scheme. Permanent position with good salary.
Write giving details of your age, experience and qualifications to Mr S Waller, R W Fothergill & Co, 202 High Street, Twyford TD1 5AT

Fig 15.2

ity as general secretary of Compton Community Association inviting the mayor and mayoress of Twyford to attend the Association's pantomime *Cinderella* to be held in the main hall at the Community Association at 1930 hrs on Friday 8 February 19–. The proceeds are in aid of the mayor's appeal fund.

b You have received the agenda for the next sports committee of Compton Community Association which is to take place on Thursday 14 February 19– at 1930 hrs. Unfortunately this is your evening class night and you are unable to attend. Write a letter of apology to the secretary.

4 You are employed by James & Brewster. You are looking after the telephone switchboard and at 1030 today receive the following telephone call:

'Hello, this is Mrs Jane Simpson. Is Mr Martin Brewster in please?'
You reply: 'No I am sorry, he has had to go out.'
'I see,' says Mrs Simpson. 'Do you think you could give him an urgent message as soon as he returns?'
'Certainly, Mrs Simpson.'
'Will you tell him that I cannot make my 12 o'clock appointment with him today because my train has been cancelled due to industrial action.'
'Of course.'
'You had better remind him that the deadline for publication is 30 November, so it is

vital I see him soon to discuss the article he is writing for our magazine.'

'Yes, of course,' you reply. 'May I have your address and telephone number please Mrs Simpson.'

'I haven't got a telephone,' answers Mrs Simpson, 'and Mr Brewster knows my Cookham, Berkshire address. Goodbye.'

'Goodbye, Mrs Simpson.'

a Write out the message on a telephone message form.

b When Mr Brewster sees the message he asks you to suggest a speedy way of replying to Mrs Simpson. Which method of communication would you recommend? Give reasons for your choice.

c Describe how a fax machine provides a suitable method of communication between branch offices in this country and overseas.

5

a You are Miss K Johnson, a sales order clerk at head office. Today you have received the following message on the telephone answering machine.

'This is John Argyle of J A Construction, 128 Southern Road, E6.

I want Peter Davison to call on me sometime next week, the middle will do. I want to discuss the new lines in your recent leaflet. I think it would also be useful if your technical adviser could call at the same time. Ask Peter Davison to ring me for an appointment, my number is 0171 486 3392. I am on extension 42.'

Compose a memorandum to be sent from you to the area manager, Mr P Davison, region ref 481, giving details of the telephone message and telling Mr Davison that John Tample, the technical adviser, is on holiday next week but will be available the following week.

b When writing a letter what are the correct complimentary closes for:
i   Dear Sir
ii Dear Mr Brown?

c Give four items of information you would expect to find on a company's letter heading apart from the company name.

6

a State, giving reasons, the most appropriate British Telecom service to use in the following situations. The firm does not have its own electronic mailing facilities.
i   A detailed engineering plan, at present in Belfast, is required at Head Office in London within the hour.
ii A firm in Australia requires immediate written confirmation of an order.
iii An interview arranged for the following day has to be postponed. It is 6 pm and the applicant has no telephone.
iv A surveyor on site is required to return to the site office immediately.
v   An emergency meeting of all Branch managers is to be arranged for tomorrow morning.
vi The sales office needs to be able to speak to a representative travelling by car at a moment's notice.

b Telephone charges for the quarter are very high. Draw up a list of six rules for the economical use of the telephone to be followed by all staff.

c Your employer is making a business trip to Holland. Name three different ways in which he could obtain information about flights to Holland from Heathrow, and give one advantage and one disadvantage for each.

7 In this assignment assume that you are employed with Paul Grant at the Westshire County Council. Miss Lucille Potter of 142 Walker Avenue, Twyford, Westshire, TD8 7LM has applied for a vacancy as a text processing operator and Mrs J Atkins, the senior administrative officer in the Youth Service section, has asked you to arrange for her to attend for an interview at 1030 hrs the day after tomorrow. You are unable to communicate with her by telephone and decide to send a telemessage. Prepare the message which you would send.

8 Refer to your organisation chart for Systems Furniture plc. Suggest with reasons the most appropriate means of communication for:
a a detailed financial document to be delivered the same day to the Welsh representative;
b an urgent telephone call received for Mr R

Weller while he is not in his office but is touring the factory with visitors;

c a request by Mrs P A Bloom for a file from the central filing room;

d a message to a person in Sheffield (not on the telephone) cancelling an appointment arranged for the day after tomorrow;

e an urgent order from the buying department to a firm in New York;

f a congratulatory message to Miss T A Green on the occasion of her wedding;

g conveying input information from branches to the firm's central computer at head office;

h discussion by senior executives of a new project;

i a confidential discussion between Mr Lawes and Mr Benney.

9 You work in the sales department of F C Equipment, Bisley.

a Using the telex message in Fig 15.3 and the price list in Fig 15.4 compose a telex message in reply to Foster Products Ltd on a telex message form. Delivery is 10–14 days, carriage paid.

b Describe how a call is made using the telex system.

c What is the main advantage of telex over:
  i   the telephone
  ii letters?

10 Write a fax message from one of your local companies to Systems Furniture plc stating that four AS1 desks were delivered to your premises today by mistake instead of four AS3 desks which were ordered (Order No A432967). Unfortunately the error was discovered after the van driver had left. Mark the fax 'urgent' and ask them to replace the desks at the earliest possible date as they are required for a new office development which is due to be completed in one week's time.

11 Mr S Waller, a partner at R W Fothergill & Co, has expressed concern about the number of errors he has discovered in legal documents after the checking has been done. He has suggested to you that the 'Hints for efficient proof-reading' on page 143 of *Office Procedures* should be incorporated in a memo to all staff involved in checking to assist them in this work and to stress the importance of the task. The extract has been typed on a word processor in Fig 15.5 and you are required to check it and mark any necessary corrections in the margin.

12 Proof-read the printed customer records in Fig 15.6 with the correct details given in Fig 5 on page xviii.

13 You receive the following telephone call from Katherine Brown of Brown & Smith, Importers.

```
859157  BISLEY G
81521  FOSTER G

TLX NO 888/IJS
DATE 15.5
RE TIMED 2.00

PLS SUPPLY CURRENT PRICES AND DEL'Y ON THE FOLLOWING ITEMS:

6 X 4 1DRAWER CARD INDEX CAB'S
8 X 5 2 DRAWER CARD INDEX CAB'S
PLANFILE CAB COMPLETE A0 SIZE 10 DRAWER
2 DRAWER FOOLSCAP FILING CAB WITH LOCK

REGARDS    IRIS SLOAN

81521  FOSTER G
859157  BISLEY G
```

Fig 15.3

CARD INDEX CABINETS

		ISO Ref	Will accept card sizes	£
FCB 13	Single Drawer Card Index Cabinet		5" x 3"	10.33
FCB 14	Single Drawer Card Index Cabinet	A6	6" x 4"	12.14
FCB 15	Single Drawer Card Index Cabinet	A5	8" x 5"	13.38
FCB 16	Single Drawer Card Index Cabinet		5" x 8"	14.46
FCB 20	Single Drawer Card Index Cabinet	B5	10" x 8"	18.02
FCB 26	Single Drawer Card Index Cabinet	A4	11¾" x 8¼"	20.19
FCB 21a	Extra for Individual Lock per cabinet drawer			1.87
FCB 23	Double Drawer Card Index Cabinet		5" x 3"	19.36
FCB 24	Double Drawer Card Index Cabinet	A6	6" x 4"	22.74
FCB 25	Double Drawer Card Index Cabinet	A5	8" x 5"	25.34
	Compressor plates: 5" x 3", 6" x 4", 8" x 5"			0.62
	5" x 8", 10" x 8", A4			0.81

Stands available on legs or castors

PLAN FILE CABINETS

FCB 31	Plan File Cabinet complete	10 Drawer Double Elephant	356.16
FCB 32	Plan File Cabinet complete	10 Drawer Antiquarian	408.16
FCB 33	Plan File Cabinet complete	10 Drawer AO	378.52
FCB 34a	Dividers for AO Drawers	*Price each*	0.70
	Rec. Quantity for A1 = 3: A2 = 7: A3 = 11: A4 = 19:		
FCB 35	All plinths		19.02
FCB 36	All Tops		21.86
FCB 37	Extra for Lock per five drawer section		23.27
FCB 38	Plan File Cabinet complete	5 Drawer Double Elephant	198.52
FCB 39	Plan File Cabinet complete	5 Drawer Antiquarian	224.52
FCB 40	Plan File Cabinet complete	5 Drawer AO	209.70

FILING CABINET DRAWER SERIES

2F	2 Foolscap Filing Drawers	Nonlock	55.30
		Locking	59.92
1F3	1 Foolscap Filing Drawer and 3–3¾" Drawers	Nonlock	49.15
		Locking	55.30
F6	6–3¾" Drawers	Nonlock	49.15
		Locking	55.30

E & OE

Fig 15.4

'I have just been lunching with Sam Lee, your Computer Manager, and promised to let him have the name of a computer package we were talking about. He said he needed the information as soon as possible. I've looked it up and it is called Tactic. He knows my telephone number.'

As you put the phone down, you notice the time is 1620. You have run out of message pads and can't leave the office. Draw up a telephone message sheet and use it to pass on the information.

(PQ OP1)

Scenario

The following scenario relates to Task 14.

H & P Office Equipment & Supplies is an expanding company engaged in the manufacture and distribution of a wide range of high quality office furniture. It also has the franchise for an internationally recognised range of office equipment. As well as selling throughout the United Kingdom, H & P also export their office furniture to several countries in Europe, using their own vehicles.

The company occupies a large factory and warehouse site from which it distributes all its goods. Its office address, where its showrooms are also located, is 24–26 Preston Road, PLYMOUTH, PL3 6PX. The telephone number is 01752 592562 and the Fax number is 01752 421333.

CHECKING PRINTOUTS AND TYPESCRIPT

A document, dispatched to a customer, or client, with undetected errors not only creates a poor impression of the organisation but can create seriuos problems. Checking (or proof reading as it is sometimes called) is therefore of great importance and cannot be stressed too much. The following hints for efficient proof reading might help you in this work:

* the printed copy must be checked word for word with the original – if possible, do this with another person: one person reading fromthe original and the other person checking the printed copy

* concentrate in checking the make-up of each word or set of figures – it is impossible to check accuracy by skimming through phrases or sentences

* at the same time as looking for errors, check that the content makes sence to you

* watch out for these errors – indicated by the following numbers in Figure 15.5:

  1 typographical errors

  2 spelling errors

  3 punctuation errors

  4 grammatical errors

  5 incorect use of capital letters

  6 mis-reading figures (when there are totals check that these are accurate)

  7 transposition of words

  8 ommissions

Fig 15.5

SYSTEMS FURNITURE plc
Customer Records (Extract)

Name	*Address*	*ID No*	*A/C Balance at 1 January 19—*
Computerland plc	Avonmouth estate 14 Southmeed Road Clifton Westshire TD4 2AP	100	£200.00 Dr

Terms: Net cash 2 months after delivery –
carriage paid
50% trade discount

| R W Fothergill & Co | 202 High Street
Twyford
Westshire TD1 5AT | 101 | |

Terms: Net cash 2 months after delivery – Carraige paid
10% trade discount

| R L Kennedy Ltd | 100 Wellington Street
Fishponds
Bristol BL7 9BQ | 102 | £50.00 Dr |

Terms: Net cash one month after invoice date
Carriage paid
5% trade discount

| P W Moore & Sons | Imperail House
14 Oxford Street
Southampton SO3 2MG | 102 | |

Terms: Net cash 14 days after invoice date
Carriage paid
7½% trade discount

| OP Electronic Services | OP House
PO Box 19
Bracknell
Berks RG21 3PT | 104 | |

Terms: Net cash within one month after delivery
10% trade discount

Fig 15.6

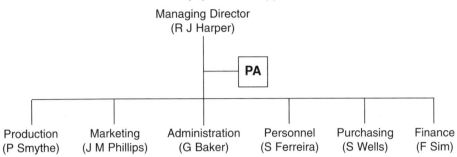

H & P Office Equipment & Supplies

Managing Director
(R J Harper)

PA

| Production (P Smythe) | Marketing (J M Phillips) | Administration (G Baker) | Personnel (S Ferreira) | Purchasing (S Wells) | Finance (F Sim) |

Fig 15.7

Its structure is a simple departmental one as indicated in the chart in Fig 15.7. The names of departmental heads are shown in brackets.

You work in the Personnel Department which is currently engaged in organising interviews for new posts within H & P.

14 The following four candidates are to be invited for interview for the position of Secretary in the Marketing Department:

Jill St Ives
Simon Stansfield
Ana Patel
Rosalyn Petrie

Interviews will take place two weeks from today and you are required to make the arrangements.

a Draft a letter to be sent to the candidates inviting them to attend for interview. (It will be produced on a word processor by the department typist.) All candidates will initially be seen together at 1030 hrs and will have the opportunity to look around the factory site. Skills tests will also take place in the mornings with formal interviews after lunch. You should enclose such details as you consider necessary, bearing in mind that only one of the candidates lives locally.

b Prepare a brief diagrammatical description of the Marketing Department as one of the enclosures. You should clearly indicate the main sections into which the marketing func-

tion is split.

c The interview panel will consist of Mrs Ferreira, Miss Shirley Tonks from the Distribution Section and the Administration Manager. Prepare a memo notifying them of the arrangements and enclosing copies of the application forms. Candidates are to be interviewed in reverse alphabetical order.

(PQ OP2)

15 Underwoods Biscuits Ltd are seeking ways of expanding their sales, especially in foreign markets.

a Explain how the following might assist in providing more effective communication with potential foreign customers, giving two examples in each case:
i   a telephone answering machine
ii telex
iii fax
iv electronic mail
v   a postal service

b List the steps you would take to make an international telephone call.

(PQ OP2)

16 In order to increase office productivity, it has been decided by the management team to introduce modern office technology. At present only electronic typewriters are in use. Select one item of modern office equipment which will provide a more speedy and efficient method for each of the following:

a written communication;

b spoken communication;

c mail handling.

Write a simple report for management stating how each piece of equipment you select would improve the efficiency of the office.

(PQ OP2)

▶ COMPUTER/WP TASKS

17

a The Mayor of Twyford will be opening new showrooms for Systems Furniture plc at their Head Office on Monday 1 February 19– at 1100. You have been asked by Mr W Morris, the Company Secretary, to send individual letters of invitation to the opening ceremony to all of the prospective customers who signed the visitors' book at the recent Furniture Exhibition and also to all existing customers. Draft an appropriate letter of invitation and type it on a word processor.

b Produce a copy of Fig 15.5 in Task 11 (checking printouts and typescript) on your word processor. Use a spelling check facility to identify any spelling or typing errors.

▶ WORK EXPERIENCE TASKS

18 Work in the buying department:

- receive and give messages:
    - hand-written
    - typewritten
    - by fax
    - by telex
- write business letters and memos
- proof-read printed and typewritten material
- distribute incoming messages to staff
- file copies of incoming and outgoing messages and correspondence

Assess your work in these tasks against the following NVQ performance criteria

ELEMENT 7.1   Respond to correspondence

(Level 2)

Performance criteria

a Correspondence received for own reply is correctly identified.

b Correspondence received outside own responsibility is routed promptly to correct person.

c The speed, mode and cost of the reply reflect its urgency and importance.

d The correct meaning and tone of the response are accurately conveyed by the language and grammar used.

e Response is accurate, clear and in the style of the organisation.

f Copies of correspondence and replies are stored in accordance with organisational procedures.

g Procedures for the security and confidentiality of data are in accordance with organisational requirements.

ELEMENT 7.2   Prepare a variety of documents

(Level 2)

Performance criteria

a Instructions are understood.

b Completed documentation meets the requirements of the workplace.

c Layout, spelling, grammar and punctuation are consistent and in accordance with conventions and house style.

d Corrections, when appropriate, are unobtrusive.

e Security and confidentiality of information is maintained.

f Copies and originals are correctly collated and routed, as directed.

g Where work is not achievable within specified deadlines reasons are promptly and
accurately reported.

h Work is achieved within agreed deadlines.

ELEMENT 8.1   Receive and transmit information electronically
(Level 2)

Performance criteria

a The most appropriate transmission system,
in relation to urgency, cost and security, is
selected.

b The equipment selected is correctly used
as laid down in operating instructions.

c Material is prepared accurately and correctly for transmission.

d Information is transmitted to correct location within required deadlines.

e Outgoing and incoming communications
are dealt with in accordance with approved
organisational procedures.

f Incoming information is promptly routed to
correct location.

g Security and confidentiality procedures conform to organisational requirements.

h Any faults are promptly rectified or
reported.

Unit 16
Mail services

1 You are responsible for preparing the mail for despatch at R W Fothergill & Co. Select an appropriate postal service for each of the following items and complete the relevant form/envelope.

a A letter to Mr R W French, 21 River Park Road, Twyford, Westshire TD4 3BR. Proof of delivery may be required in court.

b A letter to Mrs B A Smallwood, 110 Grove Road, Twyford, Westshire TD6 3LB which is urgent and must be delivered the next day.

c £50 in notes to be sent to Miss J Hobson, 24 Bath Road, Reading, Berks RG21 2BY.

d Books weighing 2kg valued at £60 to be sent to Law Stationers plc, 182 Duncan Terrace, London N1 5BX.

e Letters to Buckle, Frampton & Co, 129 Regent Grove, Leamington Spa, Warwickshire CV14 3AT and Tompkins, Long & Parkinson, 113 Dale Street, Liverpool L69 3DJ not urgent but proof of posting is required.

2 You are asked to explain the work of the mailroom to a student on a work experience scheme visiting Systems Furniture plc. How would you describe the use which would be made of the labels a to e?

a

b

c

d

e

3 You are employed in the mailroom of Systems Furniture plc.

a It is your responsibility today to deal with the documentation and calculate the postage for the parcels, registered mail and recorded delivery mail. Refer to current postal rates to complete the relevant forms and calculate the total postage for: (i) standard parcels; (ii) recorded delivery (1st class post) and (iii) registered letters for the items in Fig 16.1.

b Can you find out when it would be advisable

Name	Address	Packet	Weight	Value £
Baxters Ltd	22 Kilburn Place, London NW6 4LT	parcel	3kg	–
R W Cole	12 Station Rd, Sutton Coldfield SC9 3AR	registered	250g	400
Carpet Supply Co	31 Highland Place, Bath BH2 3AS	recorded delivery	50g	10
J Sampson	PO Box 19, Paxton Place, Twyford, Westshire TD3 9TP	parcel	4½kg	–
Fairway Fabrics plc	101 Hadrians Lane, London NW1 4AS	recorded delivery	120g	20
R W Blake & Co	100 High Street, Shepperton, Middlesex TW15 9BG	recorded delivery	40g	5
Deluxe Weavers Ltd	Dept RM4, St Pauls Road, Margate, Kent CT8 3DP	registered plus	150g	1250
L W Docherty	120 Market St, Watford, Herts WD2 19AL	parcel	1½kg	–
Wales Tourist Board	Dept V3, PO Box 1, Cardiff CF1 2XN	registered plus	300g	750

Fig 16.1

to take out insurance against consequential loss?

c Mr Pratt, the office manager, has asked you whether you think it would be worth hiring a private box at the Twyford post office. What would be the advantages to the firm?

d Mrs Fisher asks you to post an urgent letter. The post has already been delivered to the post office which is now closed. Describe the action you would take and the service you would use.

4 Amanda Jackson, the assistant secretary of Compton Community Association, has been asked to despatch a parcel of costumes used at the recent pantomime to a firm in Birmingham. The value is in the region of £100. She wants to know whether she should use recorded delivery or the compensation fee parcel service. Advise Amanda giving your reasons for the service chosen.

5 Elaine Brookes of the Brookes Office Services Agency is often requested to advise on the use of the Royal Mail and Parcelforce mail services. She has asked you to open a file on the subject and to enclose all of the current leaflets giving information about post office services.

a What leaflets and books would you collect for the file?

b Mrs Brookes has heard about some new direct mail marketing and response services offered by Royal Mail. She would like you to find out more about these new developments.

c The Royal Mail and Parcelforce offer a range of contractual services for large businesses, eg they have Mailsort. What are the benefits of this programme? What other contractual services are offered? How do contractual services differ from those offered to the general public?

d Is the Parcelforce parcel service cheaper and more efficient than the other organisations offering delivery services? What other organisations could Brookes Office Services use for the delivery of parcels?

Supply the answers to these questions in a memo addressed to Mrs Brookes.

6 You work in the Education Department's Mailroom at Westshire County Council and are required to select appropriate forms to use (from the appendix) for each of the following items of mail. Complete the forms for Westshire County Council where necessary.

a A parcel of books to be sent to the Headmaster, Barnsdale School, Stratton Road, Rushmore, Westshire RE9 4AS. The parcel weighs 3kg and is valued at £250.

b An examination certificate to be returned to Miss Monica Roberts, 132 Hillcrest Road, Twyford, Westshire TD8 4CR.

c An urgent letter which must be delivered the

next day to the Director, Westgate Polytechnic, Western Lane, Wilton, Westshire WN6 7AP.

d Letters in which evidence may be required of the date of posting to Ultrasonic Ltd, Newton Industrial Estate, Stockton-on-Tees, Cleveland CD8 3ZX and PR Designs plc, 141 North Bridge Road, Southampton SO3 1FH.

7 Beautaid Co Ltd, 23-25 High Road, Clevedon, Avon AV4 8ER, is organising a competition as part of an advertising campaign.

a 20 posters are to be delivered urgently by Datapost to Brampton Department Store, Brampton, Kent KT2 4HJ. Complete and sign the datapost form. Office number is R/6943/6.

b The prizes to be despatched include:
   i a gold necklace (value £250)
   ii a cut-glass flower vase (value £55)
   iii 100 individual theatre tickets (proof of delivery required).
   State, with reasons for your choice, the Royal Mail services you would choose for the despatch of the above prizes.

c Briefly describe the appropriate packing for each article, if needed, to ensure safe delivery.

8

a As a junior in the post room of a firm exporting goods abroad, you are required to calculate the cost of each of the items (i) to (iv) and give the total amount of postage for all the items, using current postal rates:
   i Three letters to Brunei each weighing 10½ grammes.
   ii Two packets to Tuvalu each weighing 53 grammes.
   iii Three letters to France each weighing 283 grammes.
   iv An order acknowledgement postcard to Brazil.

b What is Prestel? Identify two examples of how it would be of use to a businessperson.

c Name three services which Girobank plc offers to business customers and explain one of them in detail.

9

a You work for a company in the West Midlands. Using current postal rates state the cost of sending:
   i a parcel weighing 4.5kg to W Yorkshire
   ii a letter weighing 75g first class to London
   iii a letter to France weighing 30g
   iv a compensation fee parcel weighing 6.3kg to Somerset – value £70
   v a recorded delivery letter first class weighing 50g to Exeter
   vi a registered letter weighing 160g to Birmingham – value £150
   vii a parcel weighing 3.7kg to Worcestershire
   viii a letter weighing 210g to Aberdeen second class

b Explain the difference between:
   i recorded delivery and registered mail
   ii freepost and business reply service
   iii compensation fee parcels and datapost

10

a Read the items of mail shown in Fig 16.2. Which of these would need further information before being sent? Which would need forms completed?

b Write or type labels/envelopes for the following extra items of mail.
   ● Compensation fee parcel to Messrs B Wilson and Sons, 13 Glyndbourne Road, London EC3. Weight 2.75kg. Value £249. Mark clearly – 'For the attention of the Purchasing Officer'.
   ● Parcel to Wallis Supermarket, 5a Princetown Road, Eastbourne EA3 4FG. Weight 1025g. (Insert the county in the address.)
   ● Parcel to your local Marks and Spencer store. Weight 3.2kg. (*Remember to include postcode.*)
   ● Letter to Grenville and Spencer, Solicitors, 43 Tyne Road, Manchester. 1034g. Recorded delivery – first class.
   ● Letter to P Smythe, 132 Mile End Road, Edinburgh, ED5 9FD. Registered – contents worth £68.

c Complete any forms necessary for the post in (b).

d Using Royal mail leaflets, work out the postage for the items in (b) and frank the envelopes/labels.

11 Advise on the best way to send the following

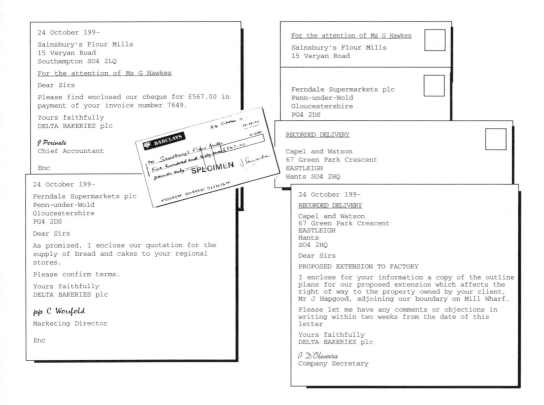

Fig 16.2

items, *using either your firm's own equipment or Royal Mail and Parcelforce services.*

a The deeds of a property being purchased by the company.

b Wages to someone without a bank account.

c A mailshot advertising a new range of products to be sent to 5000 potential customers.

d A package which must be delivered to a customer today in a town 50 miles away.

e A letter enclosing a diagram which must arrive in New York today to a firm which has all the latest technology.

f A computer package valued at £476.

g A letter cancelling an appointment for two weeks' time.

h Written confirmation of an urgent order which has already been telephoned to an organisation in Australia – an extract from their headed paper is shown in Fig 16.3.

▶ COMPUTER/WP TASKS

12 As a continuation of Task 5, use a word processor to prepare a draft letter for the Brookes Office Services Agency to send to their clients offering an advisory service on Royal Mail and Parcelforce services. Mention two or three of the new services they offer and the benefits to be gained from each of them. Say that a consultant will be pleased to call on them to give advice. Merge the letter with the following names and addresses from the clients' mailing list to produce personalised letters for Elaine Brookes to sign:

Mr R L Price, Security Equipment Sales, 80 Cubitt Street, London WC1X 8LT

Miss J Spencer, Portman Products Ltd, Unit 18, Norbury Trading Estate, Craignith Avenue, London SW16 4PX

Mr T J Berriman, TJB Enterprises Ltd, 22 St Cross Street, Hatton Gardens, London EC1N 6BR

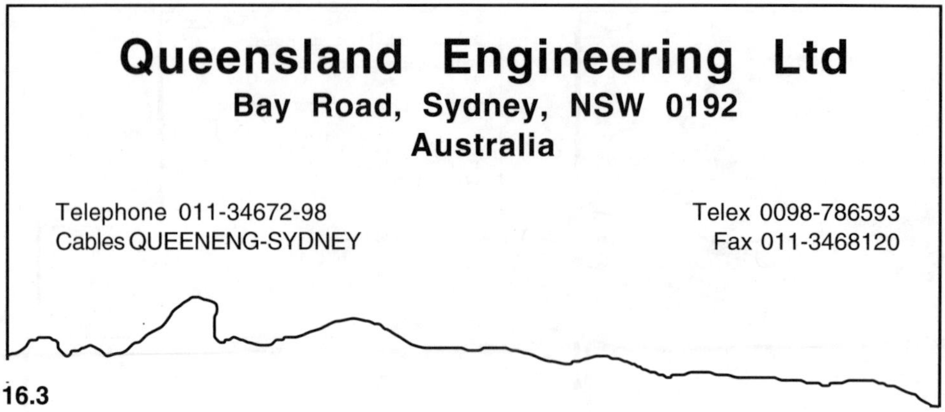

Queensland Engineering Ltd
Bay Road, Sydney, NSW 0192
Australia

Telephone 011-34672-98
Cables QUEENENG-SYDNEY

Telex 0098-786593
Fax 011-3468120

Fig 16.3

▶ WORK EXPERIENCE TASKS

13 Work in the mailroom:

- weigh letters and parcels
- select appropriate postal services
- calculate postage charges
- operate a franking machine
- select and complete the relevant forms and attach labels, as required

Assess your work in these tasks against the NVQ performance criteria

As for Unit 8 – Incoming and Outgoing Mail.

Unit 17
Receiving and assisting visitors

1 A new relief receptionist has been appointed to assist Sarah Bates at R W Fothergill & Co and you are asked to supply her with a brief guide to dealing with each of the following situations:

a receiving visitors;

b receiving a telephone call from a person making a bomb threat;

c receiving parcels at the reception desk;

d making an emergency telephone call in the event of a fire.

2 Complete *a* a register of callers and *b* visible index strips (arranged alphabetically by name of organisation) for each of the visiting cards reproduced in Fig 17.1. The times of arrival and the names of the staff they saw have been written on the cards.

3 Mr R Palmer, the deputy education officer of Westshire County Council, is concerned about the frequent accidents which are reported to him as a result of careless handling of electrical equipment in the print room. He has asked you to design a poster for the reception notice-board drawing attention to the need for safe practices when using electrical equipment. He would like you to use your imagination in designing the poster in such a way that it is eye catching and vividly portrays the consequences of ignoring such safety regulations.

MIDLAND BANK plc

196 High Street
Twyford TD3 4AP

S R Collingham
Manager   *1030*
Tel 0193 323 3146   *R P Lodge*

TWYFORD BUSINESS MACHINES

John Spencer
Sales Representative

329 Castle Lane
Twyford TD4 3LM   *1045*
(0193) 212 8196   *K. Pratt*

Joan M Brooks
Training Adviser
Manpower Services Ltd
112 Church Close
Twyford   *1015*
TD4 9RP   *P S Adams*
(0193) 316 7146

RLU (HEATING) LTD
Industrial and Domestic Heating Engineers

29 Compton Road
Twyford TD4 9TS
Tel: 0193-126-7892
P Baker   *1200*
Works Manager   *R. Weller*

WOODSIDE JOINERY
Highclass purpose built joinery

J R Norman
General Manager

4 East Street   *0930*
Shawford TD19 4RS   *K Ash*
(0193) 916 8124

GRANADA STATIONERS (WHOLESALE) LTD
Specialists in office stationery, carbons and ribbons

23 Southern Way
Compton
Westshire TD19 4LS
Tel: Compton 391487   *1115*
J R Manning   *R. Fisher*
Sales Manager

Fig 17.1

4

a On a reception register enter the following details of callers in the order in which they came to your firm on 10 May 19–. Use the 24-hour clock system.

> At 11.45 am Mr C Jones of Byway Products called to see Mr Alan Parker. Mr Parker was engaged so he was seen by Mr David South in purchasing. At 2.15 pm Mr P Watt from Jason Enterprises called and was seen by Fred Jarvis in sales. At 4.20 pm Mr Colin Sawyer of Trimfile Ltd called to see Mr Paul Jarrowe in purchasing – he was seen by Mr Jarrowe. At 10.40 am Mrs Jane Scott of Coach Services called to see Mr P Davies in transport – she was seen by Mr L Evans.

b You are about to change from being receptionist to take up another post in the organisation. Draw up a list of the three main qualities you would expect the new receptionist to possess, giving reasons for your choice.

5 Six callers at the reception office have today left visiting cards and these are reprinted in Fig 17.2. In order that follow-up visits may be arranged two tasks must be undertaken.

a Copy the data boxes in Fig 17.3 and transfer relevant information to these boxes, printing one letter in each and leaving one space between words.

b Prepare visible index strips at the foot of the data boxes where a first entry has already been made.

c Then list any other information which although not appearing on visiting cards may be obtainable from a firm's headed notepaper.

6

a Owing to the unexpected absence of the receptionist, the member of staff who has carried out reception duties has typed out notes covering what happened during the morning. Using a reception register and an appointment book make the entries as necessary in the relevant books.

> **Notes – Reception** 6 March 19– morning
> Mr Pearson from Wells, Turner & Partners arrived 9.30 am to see Mr Olsen, Chief Designer.
> Miss Rowles came to see Typing Pool Supervisor. When she left she made a further appointment for next Monday at 9.30 am. (She arrived at 9.40 am today.)
> Mr Edwards telephoned to make an appointment to see the Security Officer at 2.30 pm next Wednesday.
> Mr Kenwood arrived at 9.45 am for his appointment with Mr John. Because Mr

L. Jarrowe *Representative* Praxiteles Clinton Tel: 0122-424 821 Wilts Extension 139	Your next journey? Let EUSTACE COACHES carry your cares away *Quotations* *from:* P. N. TAYLER X40 The Wrekin, PNT Pollworthy, Som. . . . 'phone 0122-347 415	**BASSON ENGINEERING** G. Clees 0122-361 400 (ext. 101) Charlton-le-Street Dorset
Introducing *M. E. Houghton* of PRIDDY & CO. *Industrial Consultants* Keynesfield, Avon Tel. 0122-223 451 (ext. 22)	Phone: 0122-339 455 **LENNOX BROS.,** Daxford, Dorset *for Office Management* Presented by Miss P. R. DAWKINS Office ext. 59	*J. A. Milton* *Area Representative for* R LACY ASSOCIATES presents his compliments Address: Underdown Court, Brockleigh, Glos. Telephone: 0122-193 919

Fig 17.2

Name of firm	⎣⏐⏐⏐⏐⏐⏐⏐⏐⏐⏐⏐⏐⏐⏐⏐⏐⏐⏐⎦	Name of firm	⎣⏐⏐⏐⏐⏐⏐⏐⏐⏐⏐⏐⏐⏐⏐⏐⏐⏐⏐⎦
Representative	⎣⏐⏐⏐⏐⏐⏐⏐⏐⏐⏐⏐⏐⏐⏐⏐⏐⏐⏐⎦	Representative	⎣⏐⏐⏐⏐⏐⏐⏐⏐⏐⏐⏐⏐⏐⏐⏐⏐⏐⏐⎦
Telephone	⎣⏐⏐⏐⏐⏐⏐⏐⏐⏐⏐⏐⏐⏐⏐⏐⏐⏐⎦	Telephone	⎣⏐⏐⏐⏐⏐⏐⏐⏐⏐⏐⏐⏐⏐⏐⏐⏐⏐⎦
Ext no	⎣⏐⏐⏐⎦	Ext no	⎣⏐⏐⏐⎦
Date	⎣⏐⏐⏐⏐⎦	Date	⎣⏐⏐⏐⏐⎦

Fig 17.3 form continues with repeated fields: Name of firm, Representative, Telephone, Ext no, Date (three rows of paired blocks), followed by ruled lines.

AMBROSIA LTD | T Thompson - Pyper 0122 555 283 X07

Fig 17.3

John is away ill, he was seen by Mr Davies. A party of overseas visitors arrived at 10.00 am. They were met by the Managing Director. The person in charge of the party was Mr Pedersen.

Mrs Roseberry telephoned for an appointment to see the Canteen Manageress a week today at 3.10 pm. She is a representative from Finerfoods Plc.

b Fig 17.4 is an example of an employee's work pass.
  i State the purpose of such a document.
  ii What arrangements may be made to identify visitors once they have been checked in by the receptionist?

7

a Your duties as receptionist at Cartwright and Press, an advertising agency, include receiving visitors. You are frequently presented with business visiting cards by callers to the firm.
  i List three items of information which would appear on a business visiting card.
  ii State three ways in which the receptionist would make use of a business visiting card to assist in carrying out duties.
b Four visitors have made arrangements to call on your firm on Tuesday 23 June. Complete an appointments book with the following details.

  Mr J Jenkins, Acme Photocopiers Ltd, Watford, to see Sales Manager at 1030 hrs.

ALPHA WORKS LTD

WOOD STREET

EALING

TELEPHONE 0181 - 789 4560

Name   ROGER D OWEN

Dept   PERSONNEL DEPARTMENT

Card no.   PD 763

Signature   *Roger D Owen*

Authorised by   *AW*   Expiry date   SEPTEMBER 19

Fig 17.4

Ms P Evans, 135 Linden Close, Ruislip, to see Personnel Manager at 1030 hrs.

Mr A O'Hara, 23A Highgate Flats, Ickenham, to see Personnel Manager at 0930 hrs.

Miss I Gattaura, Watford Observer, Watford, to see Managing Director at 1100 hrs.

c Complete and sign a telephone message form using the information received from the following phone call at 1630 hrs.

'Hello, Cartwright and Press? Listen I'm phoning from a call box at Heathfield Hospital and I haven't any more change. My husband has an interview with you tomorrow at 9.30 but he has broken his wrist and has got to go back to hospital tomorrow morning to have an X-ray. Can he come for interview in the afternoon instead? Could you ring him – the number is Ickenham 984326 – but we won't be back from the hospital until at least 7 o'clock tonight ... I've run out of money. Goodbye.'

8 The Receptionist is sick and you are asked to take over the Reception Desk. You cannot find the Reception Register, but in the in-tray there are two lists showing expected visitors:

Callers expected this morning

9.00 Peter Brown of Brown & Smith

10.00 Jane Grace of PCL materials

Karen Page

Accounts

Visitors for Mrs Black

Mrs Black has invited applicants for the post of Junior Secretary for a preliminary interview this morning.

Carol Jones   9.45

Denise Griffiths   10.15

As Mrs Black is away, I'll see them.

John Peterson

Personnel Manager

a Draw up a Reception Register.

b Enter details of callers in the register. Assume that all visitors arrive on time.

(PQ OP1)

9 A new trainee receptionist is starting today.

a Prepare a checklist explaining briefly ways in which a good image of the organisation can be ensured.

b Draft a notice to be placed either by the fax or telex machine explaining how either would be used to send and receive messages, paying particular attention to security aspects.

(PQ OP2)

10 Underwoods is a small family business and customers and suppliers know the staff well. They walk in and out of the factory and offices freely. Recently there have been several unexplained breaches of security and the Managing Director considers that there should now be more control over who is in the factory and offices.

a Suggest four steps which could be taken to control the movement of visitors.

b Suggest steps which could be taken to prevent confidential information in documents and computer files being leaked to unauthorised people – two steps for documents and two steps for computer files.

c What would you say to a visitor who asks you for some information which is of a confidential nature?

(PQ OP2)

11 Security is an important aspect in the management of organisations.

a Identify three specific systems which may be used by a security-conscious company.

b Briefly explain any one of the systems you have identified.

c Devise a checklist which office staff (both clerical and secretarial) should work to in order to safeguard confidentiality.

(PQ OP2)

12 In view of the rapid increase in the number of visitors to Pinder & Moore in recent months the Managing Director wishes to improve the reception procedures and to tighten up on security. Draft guidelines on dealing with the following:

a Callers with an appointment.
b Casual callers.
c Difficult and angry callers.
d Company security measures.

(PQ OP2)

13 Your company has recently expanded and needs a full-time receptionist to deal with the increased number of visitors.

a Draw up a five-point guide on the way to deal with visitors coming into the reception. Give reasons and use numbered points.

b Prepare a sheet for visitors to fill in when they enter and leave the company. This is for approval by the Manager so only the headings are necessary at this stage.

(PQ OP1)

14 You work at Salter Snacks Ltd (see case study scenario). You are asked to be responsible for the reception area during the absence of the full-time receptionist.

a Explain the duties that might be performed by the receptionist in taking responsibility for the security of the reception area. Give examples where appropriate.

b Explain the advantage of a telephone answering machine to Salter Snacks. Describe the features available that might assist Sarah when her work takes her away from the office.

c Prepare a message to be recorded on the telephone answering machine.

d You overhear the following conversation. Make constructive comments.

> Receptionist: *'Hello.'*
> Caller: *'Is that Salter Snacks Ltd?'*
> Receptionist: *'Yes it is.'*
> Caller: *'Can I speak to Tony Brown please?'*
> Receptionist: *'He's not in today.'*
> Caller: *'It is rather urgent.'*
> Receptionist: *'Could you ring back tomorrow.'*
> Caller: *'Well I'm only in this country for a few days and I want to talk about purchasing some of your products.'*
> Receptionist: *'I could try the Assistant Sales Manager for you.'*
> Caller: *'Thank you.'*
> Receptionist: (After a few minutes) *'She's not in her office either. Why don't you ring her this afternoon?'*

(PQ OP2)

15 Assume that you are the receptionist at Salter Snacks Ltd (as in the case study scenario). A party of foreign business men and women are expected today at 1100 and you have a note asking you to let Mr Baker know as soon as they arrive.

Role play the following situations, each member of your group taking the various parts of the visitors and receptionist. If possible, video the roleplay exercise.

a The foreign business executives arrive at the expected time.

b The receptionist greets the visitors and asks them to sign the register of callers.

c The receptionist telephones Mr Baker to announce their arrival.

d Mr Baker says he will collect the visitors in about ten minutes as he is 'tied up' at the moment.

e The receptionist conveys the message diplomatically to the visitors and asks them to take a seat. The receptionist gives the visitors each a badge and explains in careful English that the badges must be worn while the visitors are on the premises and handed back when they leave.

f Herr Becker then asks the receptionist to tell them something about the firm.

g The receptionist explains how the firm is run and the visitors ask questions (the receptionist must remember that the visitors do not understand English very well).

h Daniela Rossi asks for the directions to the nearest railway station as one of the party is going straight to London after the visit.

i The receptionist gives directions (assume that Salter Snacks Ltd is sited next to your college/school).

j Mr Baker arrives to collect the visitors.

► **COMPUTER/WP TASKS**

16

a It is essential for all of the secretaries at Systems Furniture plc to inform the Reception Office of the visitors they are expecting and this should be done at least one day before the visit. Suggest a system which will enable the secretaries to transmit this information direct from their word processing terminals to Jane Wilkinson, the receptionist.

b Use a word processor to type the telephone message for Task 7(*c*). What are the advantages of using a word processor for typing and distributing messages? Could you use the system recommended for (*a*)?

► **WORK EXPERIENCE TASKS**

17 Work in the reception office:
● receive callers and, where relevant, direct them to appropriate staff
● receive messages and convey them to staff concerned
● receive, connect and make telephone calls using the switchboard

● enter appointments in the visitors' appointments diary
● take care of the reception area to ensure that it is always tidy and of pleasing appearance
● update display material, charts, internal telephone index and ensure that supplies of publicity leaflets and other reading matter are available for visitors.

Assess your work in these tasks against the following NVQ performance criteria

ELEMENT 2.2   Monitor and maintain the security of the workplace
(Level 2)

Performance criteria
a Organisational security procedures are carried out correctly.
b Security risks are correctly identified.
c Identified security risks are put right or reported promptly to the appropriate person.
d Identified breaches of security are dealt with in accordance with organisational procedures.

ELEMENT 4.2   Receive and assist visitors
(Level 2)

Performance criteria
a Visitors are greeted promptly and courteously.
b The nature of the visit and the needs of visitors are identified and matched to the appropriate products, personnel or services of the organisation.
c Reception and directing of visitors is in accordance with established procedures.
d The structure, products or services of the organisation are accurately described and promoted to the visitors as appropriate.
e Methods of communication and support are suited to the needs of the visitors.
f Communication difficulties are openly acknowledged and appropriate help sought to ensure understanding.
g Difficulties in providing support to visitors are acknowledged and appropriate help sought.
h Records are complete, legible and accurate.
i Established procedures are followed for dealing with awkward or aggressive visitors.

Unit 18
Travel arrangements

1 Mr R W Fothergill, senior partner of R W Fothergill & Co, is travelling by plane to Aberdeen where he will stay for two nights, returning to London by train via Edinburgh where he will spend one night. He wishes you to:
a book his tickets;
b make reservations for travel and hotels;
c arrange for him to be taken to and from the airports and the railway stations.
How will you make these arrangements?

2 Mr R Weller, Production Manager of Systems Furniture plc, wishes to travel by train to Coventry in order to visit a factory which is situated three miles outside the city. He wishes to stay the night at a hotel and return the following morning. Draw up a checklist of the arrangements you will make for him.

3 Prepare the itinerary required in the note (Fig 18.1) from Mr P A Jones, Chief Designer at Systems Furniture plc.

4 The senior staff of the Education Department of Westshire County Council are planning to hold a one-day staff conference at the Westbrook Hotel, five miles out of Twyford. You have been asked to make arrangements to book the hotel conference room.
a What steps would you take to undertake this task?
b Draft the letter of confirmation which you would send to the Hotel.

5 Prepare the itinerary and explain what arrangements you would make for your manager, Mr Peter Clarke, to attend the International Book Fair at Frankfurt from 15–17 October 19–.

6 Your employer has to fly to New York (Kennedy Airport) on Tuesday 25 July 19–. He is to visit the Chuck Lucas Organisation, 500 5th Avenue, New York, telephone 721 6543621, on Wednesday and Muter, Levi & Gould Inc, 28th Floor, 1100 42nd Street, telephone 750 2296118, on the Thursday and Friday. He will return on the Saturday. He requires transport while in New York and he does not like to use travel agents.
a List the arrangements you would make on his behalf.
b Prepare an itinerary, using appropriate times.

7 You work at the London head office of a

Will you please prepare my itinerary for Tuesday, Wednesday and Thursday. I will meet the agents from Gatwick Airport at 1500 on Tuesday and I will take them back to the airport on Thursday at 1600. The meeting will be held in the company boardroom from 1000 to approximately 1600. On Thurday morning at 1000 I have arranged to show the agents round the works   PAJ

Fig 18.1

company of office equipment manufacturers as secretary to Mr Charles Barrington, the company's Managing Director.

Mr Barrington has to be in Manchester next Monday in time for a luncheon appointment at 1230 hrs with Mr James Dodd at the Midland Hotel. He will be returning to London on Wednesday morning, leaving Manchester about 1000 hrs. Select a good hotel in Manchester (at least three star) and reserve a room for Mr Barrington for the Monday and Tuesday evenings. He prefers a room on the quiet side of the hotel. You have arranged an appointment on Monday at 1500 hrs for Mr Barrington to see Mr R Parker of Parker Bros, 11 Portland Street and on the Tuesday you have arranged an 1100 hrs appointment with Major J Masters of Northern Electronics Ltd, 141 Accrington Road, Burnley. He will travel to Burnley by train and will be lunching with Major Masters at the Keirby Hotel at 1300 hrs. In the evening Mr Barrington has booked to attend a lecture at the Manchester Business School at 1900 hrs.

a Look up times of suitable trains and prepare Mr Barrington's itinerary for Monday, Tuesday and Wednesday.

b Write a letter to the hotel reserving accommodation and attach a copy of it to the itinerary.

8 Your employer, Mr Donald Jamieson, is shortly going on a business trip to Belgium, France, Germany, the Netherlands and Denmark. The various rates of exchange keep fluctuating and he would like you to check on today's rates against the £ sterling for each of these countries. In addition to foreign money he will need to take a number of travellers cheques. He finds the £20 units which he has used up to now on his business trips are too small for his use and asks you to ascertain what higher units of travellers cheques are obtainable. Type all the information requested, in memo form, to Mr Jamieson.

9 When travelling at home and overseas the organisation of business travel has, in the past, been carried out by staff themselves. In future it has been decided to make one person responsible for all travel arrangements.

a Prepare a list of duties and reminders for dealing with travel arrangements.

b Indicate the steps that need to be taken to ensure the smooth running of the office while a senior member of staff is away on business.

(PQ OP2)

10 The week after the reception, Jeanne Fiquet, author of a French language textbook in the new business studies series, is spending two days in France as part of a sales promotion campaign. Prepare the itinerary using the information contained in Mme Fiquet's memo to Elizabeth Berger (Fig 18.2).

(PQ OP2)

▶ COMPUTER/WP TASKS

11 In what ways can you use teletext and e-mail in your travel arrangements?

▶ WORK EXPERIENCE TASKS

12 Work in the section responsible for making travel arrangements involving communication and discussion with staff, requiring the service; travel agents; hotels; railways; airports; car-hire firms.

Assess your work in these tasks against the following NVQ performance criteria:

ELEMENT 11.1   Arrange travel for persons
(Level 2)

Performance criteria
a Instructions for travel requirements are understood.
b Travel arrangements conform to specified instructions and organisational procedures.
c A clear and accurate schedule, containing all arrangements made, is provided to the appropriate person.
d Travel documents are complete and accurate.
e Security and confidentiality procedures conform to organisational requirements.
f Arrangements are made within agreed deadlines.

MEMORANDUM

TO: Elizabeth Berger

FROM: Jeanne Fiquet   Date: (Yesterday's
                                                            date)

RE: <u>My visit to Paris</u>

I shall be flying from London City Airport on the 1130 plane to Paris (PA117), which takes about an hour. I need to be there 45 minutes before the flight leaves. As I shall have to collect some papers from the office first, could you please arrange for a car to take me to the airport. We should allow 20 minutes for the drive. I have booked to return from Paris two days later on the 1550 plane (PA118). Please arrange for a car to collect me.

I have made the following appointments.

On the first day I am meeting Marie Duval at 1530 hours in my hotel. I expect that will take an hour. I have then invited Pierre and Jacqueline Panisse to join me for dinner at my hotel at 2000 hours.

At 1030 the following morning I shall be at the Librairie Marius in La Rue Fontenay. They are arranging a special display of my book. I expect I shall be lunching with them.

I shall need to take some sales literature with me. Will this be available in French by then? I could also do with some visiting cards. Can you arrange this?

By the way, I telephoned my usual hotel and booked my accommodation at the Hotel du Cerf. Will you please confirm the booking. Please let me have an itinerary.

PS   Just a reminder – Paris time is 1 hour ahead of London.

Fig 18.2

ELEMENT 11.2   Book accommodation for a specified purpose
(Level 2)

Performance criteria

a Instructions for accommodation arrangements are understood.
b Accommodation arrangements meet specified instructions.
c A clear and accurate confirmation of all
   arrangements made is provided to the
   appropriate person.
d Security and confidentiality procedures conform to organisational requirements.
e Arrangements are completed within agreed
   deadlines.

Unit 19
Organising meetings and other events

1 Assume that you are assisting Roger Parker as Secretary of the Westshire County Council's Sports and Social Club Committee. The Chairman sends you a list of the special items to be discussed at the next meeting (two weeks today) at the Clubhouse. From these notes draw up the agenda ready to send out to members of the committee, including the items which normally appear on the agenda. The following are the notes you receive:

a We haven't decided where to have the autumn dinner or who should be our guest speaker. Ask Mrs Wright to have some suggestions ready.

b The clubhouse needs redecorating. Do we have sufficient funds to pay for it to be done or should we organise voluntary labour?

c We have to deal with applications for membership at this meeting. Remember to bring the application forms.

d Expenses have gone up so much recently that we ought to consider putting up membership subscriptions. We should discuss this so that we have our facts ready to present at the next annual general meeting.

2 Tony Miles has been given the job of organising the next disco for the youth members of the Compton Community Association. Compile a checklist of the action he will need to take to organise the event.

3 Carol Pitman will be away on holiday for the next meeting of the Management Committee of Compton Community Association and Amanda Jackson, the assistant secretary, will be required to organise the meeting.

a Supply Amanda with a checklist of the action she should take before the meeting, on the evening of the meeting and after the meeting has taken place.

b Why do you think they need a management committee for the association?

4 Refer to the agenda shown in Fig 19.1 and explain the meaning of the items 1, 2, 3, 4, 7 and 8.

5 Write the following for the minutes of a meeting:

'I suggest that we should allocate an appropriate sum for the purchase of desktop publishing equipment which would enable us to carry out our internal printing. In the long run this would be an economy.'

This suggestion, made by Mr Henderson, was proposed, seconded and agreed by the Board.

6
a What do you understand by an amendment to a motion?

b For what reason might a member of an organisation be co-opted on to a committee?

c Give one reason why a meeting might be adjourned for a few days.

d What is an ex-officio member of a committee?

e What is the purpose of a quorum?

7 The MD's secretary is away on holiday and you have been asked to arrange a Board Meeting at short notice to be held in the company's Board Room. The meeting will probably last all day.

a Make a checklist for yourself so you do not forget anything. Use the headings, Before, During, After Meeting.

b Some members of the meeting will be travel-

```
NOTICE OF MEETING

The next committee meeting of the
Community Education Committee will take
place on Wednesday 2 February 19- at 1930
at the Community Association Headquarters.

AGENDA

1 Apologies for absence
2 Minutes of the last meeting
3 Matters arising
4 Treasurer's Report
5 Proposed increase in fees
6 New courses for the summer
7 Any other business
8 Date of next meeting
```

Fig 19.1

ling from different parts of the country. Not all these people will be directors but will have been asked to attend this meeting for various reasons. What special arrangements will you make for these people?

(*PQ OP2*)

8

a Prepare a notice of meeting and an agenda for a meeting of the Canteen Committee to be held in Committee Room A on the first Monday of next month at 1000 hours. As well as the usual items include:

i price increases

ii introduction of new dishes

iii opening times.

b Explain what you understand by the following:

i Quorum

ii Ad hoc

iii Point of Order.

c Prepare a checklist of six tasks that you would perform on the day of the meeting in preparing the room.

(*PQ OP2*)

9 Elizabeth Berger has left a message on the telephone answering machine saying she is unable to be in the office today and asking you to prepare the notice and agenda of the next Board meeting which will be held in the Boardroom at 1030 hours two weeks from today. She asks you to include all the usual items plus one on "European Promotions' and one on 'Electronic Equipment'. Also to circulate to the Board the background papers regarding the European promotion campaign using a circulation slip.

a Draft the notice and agenda of the meeting.

b Complete the circulation slip.

c Write out a checklist of other things to be done:

i before the meeting

ii during the meeting.

(*PQ OP2*)

10

a At the end of the Management team meeting it is agreed that the next meeting will be held in the Boardroom one week from today's date at 1000 hours. Compile a notice convening the meeting, together with an agenda. Jane Sheridan wants an item on European markets and John Brewer wants one on office technology. Include these and all of the usual items.

b The management team chair meetings in rotation. Michael Greene will chair the next meeting. How will the chairperson's agenda differ from that of the others?

c What will Michael Greene's duties be during and after the meeting?

(PQ OP2)

11 As secretary of the firm's social club, you have been asked to prepare the Agenda for the next meeting to be held at the Clubhouse on the last day of next month at 1900 hours.

Prepare the notice and Agenda, which should include the usual items plus the purchase of a new billiards table, the Annual Party and the Football Fixtures for the next season.

(PQ OP2)

▶ COMPUTER/WP TASKS

12 Use a word processor to type the agenda in Task 1 for the Westshire County Council Sports Social Club. Explain how the word processor can be used to speed up the process of typing future agenda and for addressing the labels to members.

▶ WORK EXPERIENCE TASKS

13
a Assist in organising meetings
b draft agenda and notice of meetings
c Attend meetings and take minutes

Assess your work in these tasks against the following NVQ performance criteria

ELEMENT 12.1   Assist in arrangements for the provision of supporting facilities and materials at events
(Level 2)

Performance criteria
a The quantity, type and quality of supporting

materials is as directed.
b Equipment and materials are located to suit purpose of events within agreed deadlines.
c Instructions for the safeguarding of equipment and materials are followed.
d Facilities for persons with special needs are confirmed.

ELEMENT 12.2   Assist in arrangements for the attendance of persons at events
(Level 2)

Performance criteria
a Persons invited to attend the event are as directed.
b Accurate and complete event directions and supporting documentation are provided to persons attending, appropriate to their role and need.
c Arrangements, when required, for the transportation of persons, are appropriate and within budgetary allocation.
d The reception and routing of persons at events provides adequate support and direction.
e Attendance records are in accordance with organisational requirements.

ELEMENT 12.3   Assist in arrangements for the provision of catering services at events
(Level 2)

Performance criteria
a Arrangements for catering services are as directed.
b The needs of persons attending are identified and catered for.
c Costs of catering services are within budgetary allocation.
d Arrangements for catering services are made within agreed deadlines.
e The arrangements for catering services are in accordance with organisational requirements.
f Precautions taken with the provision of catering services provide adequate safeguarding of persons and property at events.

Unit 20
Sources of information

1

a Mrs R Fisher, the supervisor of secretarial services at Systems Furniture plc, has asked you to order the following books from Fullers Book Supplies Ltd, 192 High Street, Twyford, Westshire TD1 5AT and to add two other books which you consider to be useful for reference purposes in the secretarial support services section.

   i   *Concise Oxford Dictionary*
   ii *Roget's Thesaurus of English Words and Phrases*
   iii *Pear's Cyclopaedia*
   iv *The Secretary's Desk Book, Harrison*
   v *Black's Titles and Forms of Address*

Ascertain the prices from your library and type an order form for despatch today.

b Describe the type of information which the secretaries could obtain from each of these books.

2 Mrs Mason, the secretary to the managing director of Systems Furniture plc, has to attend to the following matters. Suggest the reference book or other source which she might wish to use for each item.

a Calculate the value in £ sterling of 50 French francs.
b Book a room at a hotel in Manchester.
c Ascertain the population of Sheffield.
d Write to the Norwegian Embassy in London.
e Write some biographical notes about the Prime Minister.
f Check the spelling and location of a small town in France.
g Send a fax message to a firm in Glasgow.
h Write a letter of enquiry to several firms selling office equipment in Twyford.

3

a What reference books would you suggest should be available at R W Fothergill & Co in the following offices?
   i   senior partner
   ii secretarial support services
   iii mailroom
   iv receptionist/telephonist
b In what ways would each of the books suggested in *a* be used?

4 Where would you go to get, or to deal with:

a a new passport;
b renewal of a motor car tax disc;
c a TV licence;
d a new cheque book;
e foreign currency for your holiday;
f a reference book not available in your office;
g finding a new job in an office;
h information about a foreign country where you will be spending your holiday;
i a new government publication;
j a query concerning your income tax allowances.

5 The advertising company for which you work constantly requires up-to-date information under the following headings:

a travel – home/abroad, by air/train/road;
b addresses and telephone numbers of clients and contacts;
c background information about countries, people and companies;
d suppliers' names and telephone numbers;
e home and overseas mailing information;
f English usage.
   i   For each heading suggest a standard reference book which could be kept in the advertising company's office and give brief details of four of them.
   ii Describe four sources of commercial information other than reference books which the company may use.

6 Which reference books would you use to find out more information about:

a R W Fothergill & Co?

b Systems Furniture plc?

c Westshire County Council?

d The Brookes Office Services Agency?

e Compton Community Association?

f Salter Snacks Ltd?

What information would you gain from these books?

7 Refer to the line graph (Fig 20.1) and bar chart (Fig 20.2) in *Office Procedures* and supply the following information in respect of the sales of Systems Furniture plc for the half-year January to June 19–:

a What were the total sales for the six-month period?

b What percentage of the total sales were the sales of executive desks?

c In which month was the greatest gap between the sales of systems desks and executive desks?

d In which months did total sales exceed £200,000?

e What were the monthly averages for total sales; systems desk sales and executive desk sales?

f Compile a line graph and a bar chart for the remainder of the year from the following figures:

	Systems desks £000	Executive desks £000
July	90	90
August	80	60
September	110	100
October	140	110
November	100	80
December	130	90

g Compare the sales results for the second half of the year with the first half:

i   Was there an increase or decrease in total sales; in systems desk sales and in executive desk sales?

ii   Now answer questions *a* to *e* in respect of the second half-year figures

8

a Elaine Brookes has to deal with several organisations in connection with the running of her new business. Name these organ-

isations and explain the nature of the business which she conducts with them.

b It is essential for local businesses to be made aware of the existence of the Brookes Office Services Agency and the services it offers. How can Elaine Brookes do this? In which of the local reference sources should the firm be featured?

c Make a list of the reference books which the Brookes Office Services Agency would need, explaining for what purposes they would be used.

9

a List four reference books that you would expect a receptionist/telephonist to have available, stating when each book would most likely be used.

b Explain briefly how information can be obtained using Prestel and give examples of the information which can be obtained from its use.

c Fig 20.1 contains a note from your employer. List the reference sources you would use to obtain the information he requires.

10

a Using the visual control board in Fig 20.2 find the information to answer the questions given below and where necessary change the board as instructed.

i   Indicate on the board, using the correct symbol, to which members you would send a programme/agenda.

ii   Mr Alun Martin telephones you to say that he will attend only the Annual General Meeting and the Annual Dinner and will not need accommodation. He will pay his fees on arrival. Add this information to the board and change the board to include any additional information that you will need to send him.

iii   How many places will be needed in the Conference during the Annual General Meeting? Assume that those attending for the full week will also attend the Annual General Meeting.

iv   How many members will require accommodation during the conference?

v   Harold Williams telephones because he has lost his papers and asks you to con-

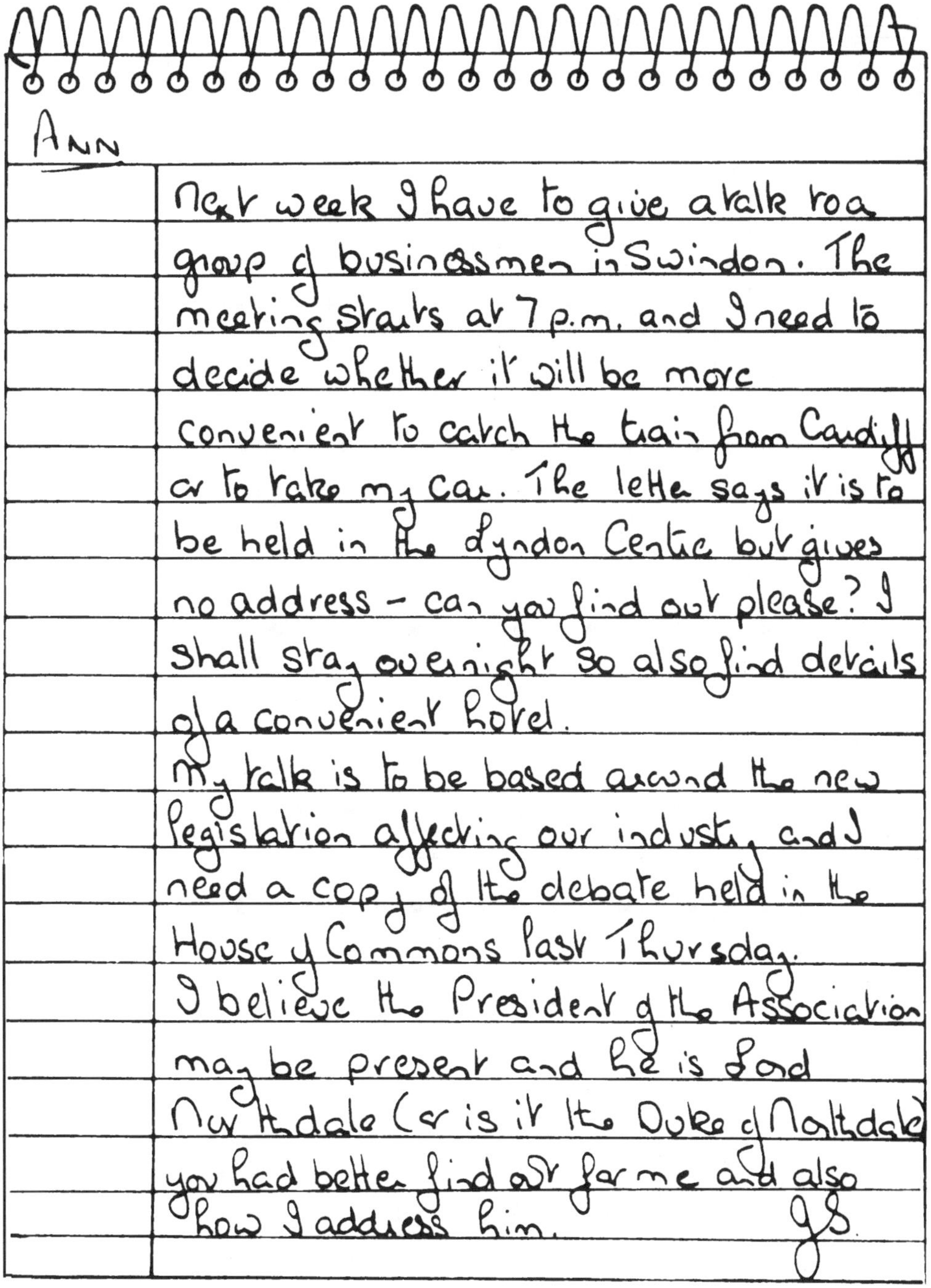

ANN

Next week I have to give a talk to a group of businessmen in Swindon. The meeting starts at 7 p.m. and I need to decide whether it will be more convenient to catch the train from Cardiff or to take my car. The letter says it is to be held in the Lyndon Centre but gives no address – can you find out please? I shall stay overnight so also find details of a convenient hotel.

My talk is to be based around the new legislation affecting our industry and I need a copy of its debate held in the House of Commons last Thursday.

I believe the President of the Association may be present and he is Lord Northdale (or is it the Duke of Northdale) you had better find out for me and also how I address him.   JS.

Fig 20.1

NAME AND REGION	Conference details	Reply	Residential	Non-residential	Full week	AGM only	Annual dinner	Programme/agenda	Travel details	Deposit paid	Full fee paid	Booked in
JOHN H BROWN (South Wales)	◀	●	●		●		●		◀	✓	✓	
PETER COX (Midlands)	◀	●	●		●		●		◀	✓	✓	
GARETH DAVIES (Bristol & West)	◀	●	●		●		■		◀	✓		
DAVID EVANS (London)	◀	●		●			●		◀	✓	✓	
JONATHON HOWELLS (Home Counties)	◀	■										
ARTHUR JAMES (Birmingham)	◀	●	●	●	●	●	●		◀	✓		
GRAHAM JOHN (Yorkshire)	◀	●				●	●		◀			
ALUN MARTIN (East Wales)	◀	×										
DANIEL MORGAN (Merseyside)	◀	●	●		●		●		◀	✓	✓	
JAMES OWEN (Devon & Cornwall)	◀	■					■		◀			
LEONARD PEACOCK (Tyneside)	◀	●	●	●	●	●	●		◀	✓	✓	
FRANK PHILLIPS (West Midlands)	◀	●	●		●		●		◀	✓		
CHRISTOPHER TAYLOR (Swindon)	◀	■										
IVOR THOMAS (Lincolnshire)	◀	●	●		●		●		◀			
TREVOR WILLIAMS (Border)	◀	×										
HAROLD WILLIAMS (Manchester)	◀	●	●		●		●		◀	✓	✓	
COLIN WOOLEY (South Eastern)	◀	●	●		●		●		◀	✓	✓	

KEY

●	ACCEPTANCES	
■	REFUSALS	
◀	INFORMATION SENT	
×	DID NOT REPLY	

Fig 20.2

firm the details by listing what he has booked for and what fees he has paid.

b i Name the British Telecom viewdata service.

ii List three types of information available by using this service.

iii Describe how such information is obtained.

11 Supply the answers to the following A-Z questions and in each case state the source of reference used:

a The meaning of the abbreviation GATT.

b The name and address of the Bishop of Durham and the correct form of address for him.

c The address and telephone number of the Financial Times.

d The fax number for Mercury Communications Limited.

e The geographical location of Baton Rouge.

f The times and flight numbers of British Airways flights leaving London (Heathrow) for New York (John F Kennedy) on a Friday morning.

g The population of Bath and the names of the chief local government executives there.

h The name, address and telephone number of two office equipment retailers in your nearest town.

i The direct mail postal services offered by Royal Mail.

j The subject of a speech given by your local MP in the House of Commons.

k The name and address of your local Euro MP.

l The current rate of exchange of US dollars against £ sterling.

m The names of the directors of one of your largest local companies.

n The name and address of a good hotel in Middlesbrough.

o Another word for indecipherable.

p Advice to a business executive visiting Pakistan.

q Biographical notes about the Chancellor of the Exchequer.

r Names and addresses of voluntary organisations in your local community.

s The address of the IMF.

t The value of 100 shares in Guinness.

u The cost of purchasing 500 Swiss francs.

v The cost of a telephone call to Australia.

w The time difference between the UK and Jamaica.

x The weather forecast for your region.

y The percentage of Britain's total trade which was with the EU for last year.

z The name of the Prime Minister of Japan.

12 The Director of Sales and Marketing wants to be able to quickly compare the sales of textbooks.

a Draw a bar chart to show the sales over a three-year period using the following information.

	1994	*1995*	*1996*
Engineering	1500	1250	1000
Business studies	2000	2250	3000
Hotel and Catering	1250	1000	1500
Foreign Languages	1250	1750	2500

b i Using the total of Business Studies textbooks sold in 1996 (see above) prepare a pie chart to show the size of markets for these books in:

Europe	1500
Africa	750
India	750

ii Express the proportions in percentage terms.

(PQ OP2)

13 The Sales Director is making a two-day visit to the North during which he will present the figures for the last three years for the sales of children's clothes at both home and overseas. He has drawn up the figures in the form of a line graph but has decided that his presentation will be more effective as a bar chart.

Using the line graph you have been given (Fig 20.3) convert it to a bar chart showing the start of the year figures for both overseas and home.

(PQ OP2)

▶ **COMPUTER/WP TASKS**

14 It is your responsibility to use teletext every day to update the following chart (Fig 20.4) of selected share prices and foreign currency rates and to produce a copy on your word processor

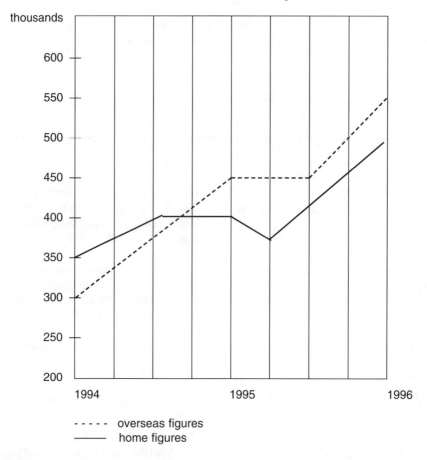

Children's clothes sales figures

thousands

- - - - - overseas figures
———— home figures

Fig 20.3

for Mr R A Lawes, Managing Director of Systems Furniture plc. Produce the copies required for today and tomorrow.

▶ **WORK EXPERIENCE TASKS**

15 Work in a business library:

- extract the relevant information from dictionaries, reference books and trade journals and transmit it in an appropriate format to staff requesting it
- use videotex to secure information
- telephone and write to organisations to obtain required information.

```
┌─────────────────────────────────────────────┐
│              DAILY DATA SHEET                 │
│                                               │
│  Date:                                        │
│                                               │
│  Share prices:          Foreign currency tourist │
│                         rates for £1:         │
│                                               │
│  Amstrad                French franc –        │
│                                               │
│  Courtaulds             German mark –         │
│                                               │
│  GEC                    Italian lira –        │
│                                               │
│  Racal                  Japanese yen –        │
│                                               │
│  Unilever               US dollar –           │
│                                               │
└─────────────────────────────────────────────┘
```

Fig 20.4

Assess your work in these tasks against the following NVQ performance criteria

ELEMENT 5.2   Supply information for a specific purpose
(Level 2)

Performance criteria
a Information requirements are understood.
b Information sources are correctly identified and accessed.
c Where available information does not match requirements, options and alternatives are identified and offered.
d Information is correctly transcribed and compiled.
e The information supplied is in an appropriate form.
f Essential information is supplied within required deadlines.
g Confidential information is disclosed only to authorised persons.

Section E

MASTER FORMS FOR USE WITH ASSIGNMENTS

PURCHASES REQUISITION				
No				
Date				
Quantity	Description	Supplier's Cat No	Purchase Order No	Supplier

Signed..   Approved..

Authorised...   Buyer

F1

ORDER

From: No

Tel: Telex:
                                               Fax:
                                               Date:

To:

Please supply:

Quantity	Description	Your Cat No	Price each £

Deliver by:

to:

....
                                               Buyer

F2

INVOICE

From: No

                                                   Fax:
Tel: Telex:

VAT Registration No   Date:

To:

Terms:

Completion of Order No   dated

Quantity	Description	Cat No	Price each £	Cost £	VAT rate %	VAT amount £

Delivered on:

          by:

F3

134

TIMEPIECES LTD
Century Works
Bridgeway
19 6HY

INVOICE NO: 7171

Tel: 012-339-5161

Fax: 012-33-7171

ORDER NO:

ORDER DATE:

DATE:

TO:

Terms 3% for monthly settlement

Quantity	Description	Cat No	Item Price £	Total Price £

TOTAL goods
LESS: 10% Trade Discount

NEW TOTAL
TOTAL Government Tax 15%

TOTAL BALANCE DUE

F4

INVOICE

No   3987/4

From: Universal Books Ltd
        Docklands House
        Wapping Wall
        London E3 4NX

Tel: 0171-481 7369   Fax: 0171-481 6511

VAT Registration No: 209 3814 86   Date:

To:

Terms:

Completion of Order No   dated

Quantity	Description	Cat No	Price each £	Cost £	Discount £	Total amount £

Delivered on: **TOTAL**
        By: **INVOICE**

F5

CREDIT NOTE

No

From:

Telex:

Tel:

Fax:

VAT Registration No

Date:

Ref: Invoice No

dated

To:

Quantity	Description	Price each £	Cost £	VAT rate %	VAT amount £

F6

STATEMENT

From:

Tel:

Telex:

Fax:

To:

Date:

Terms:

Date	Details	Ref No	Dr £	Cr £	Balance £

The last amount in the balance column is the amount owing

F7

STOCK CONTROL CARD

Item:

Stores Ref:

Location:

Maximum:

Re-order level:

Minimum:

Unit:

Date	Receipts			Issues			Balance in stock	On order			
	Quantity	Inv No	Quantity	Quantity	Reqn No	Dept/ staff		Date ordered	Quantity	Order No	Date rec'd

F8

STOCK CONTROL CARD

Ref: 0 09 9092143   Maximum: 400

Location: TOP SHELF   Minimum: 80

Item: "BUSINESS STUDIES IN THE 1990s"

Date	Ref	In	Out	Balance
5 MAR				400
10 MAR	VALLEY COLL		50	350
15 MAR	TUDOR BKSHOP		25	325
17 MAR	ORR SCH		30	295
4 APR	BUSINESS COLL		120	175
18 APR	BAKER'S		75	100
21 APR	APT		50	50
22 APR		350		400

STOCK CONTROL CARD

Ref: 0 09 9073162   Maximum: 150

Location: TOP SHELF   Minimum: 50

Item: "THE SECRETARY AT WORK"

Date	Ref	In	Out	Balance
1 FEB				150
2 MAR	DIORS BKSHOP		20	130
7 MAR	HAYES COLL		20	110
20 APR	SOUTHERNS		100	10
20 APR		150		160
25 MAY	RED HILL SCH		5	155

F9

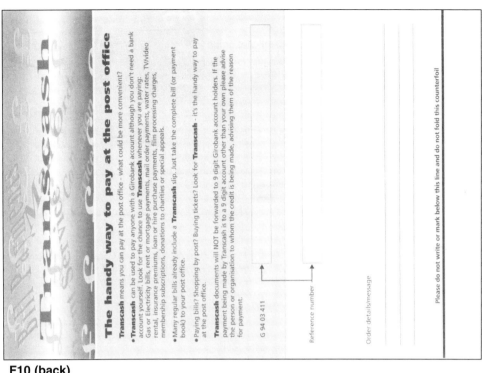

F10 (back)

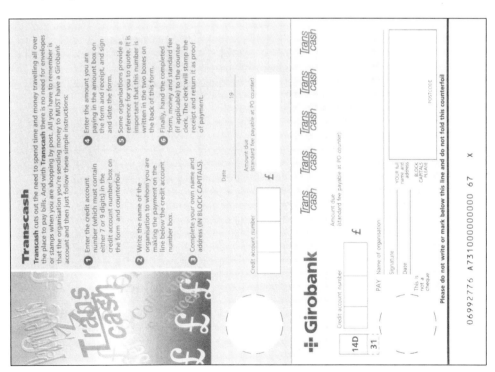

F10 (front)

F11

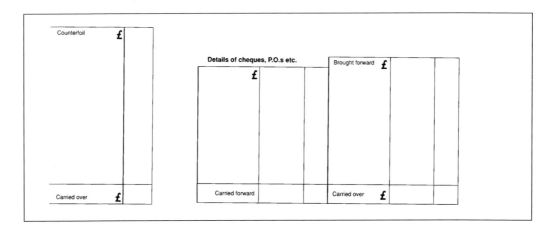

F12

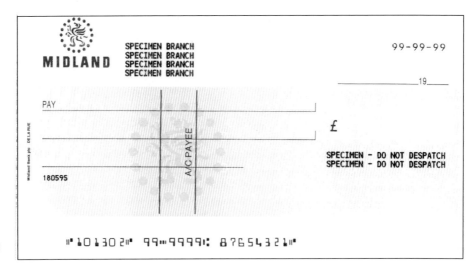

F13

Standing Order Mandate

TO **Midland Bank plc**

Date _____

Address _____

	Bank	.	Branch Title *not address*	Sorting Code number
Please pay				— — —

	Beneficiary	Account number
for the credit of		

	Date and amount of first payment		Date and frequency
†the sum of	£	and thereafter every	

	Amount in figures	Amount in words
Subsequent payments	£	

	Date and amount of last payment	
*until	£	*until you receive further notice from me/us in writing
quoting the reference		and debit my/our account accordingly.

*Please cancel any previous order in favour of the Beneficiary named above, under this reference.

*Delete as appropriate

†If the amounts of periodic payments vary they should be incorporated in a schedule overleaf.

Special instructions

Signature/s _____   _____

Title of account and
account number to be debited _____ | | | | | | | |

Note: The Bank will not undertake to
a) make any reference to Value Added Tax or pay a stated sum plus V.A.T., or other indeterminate element.
b) advise remitter's address to beneficiary.
c) advise beneficiary of inability to pay.
d) request beneficiary's banker to advise beneficiary of receipt.

1584 1

F14

From

Midland Bank plc

bank giro credit ⟁

Branch

Date

Code number	Bank & Branch	Credit account & account number	Amount
		£	

By order of
2090-9

From

Midland Bank plc

bank giro credit ⟁

Branch

Date

Code number	Bank & Branch	Credit account & account number	Amount
		£	

By order of
2090-9

From

Midland Bank plc

bank giro credit ⟁

Branch

Date

Code number	Bank & Branch	Credit account & account number	Amount
		£	

By order of
2090-9

F15

144

TO **Midland Bank plc**

bank giro credit
summary form

Branch _____ Date _____

Please distribute the bank giro credits attached as arranged with the recipients.

Our cheque for £ _____ is enclosed.

Number of Items

Customer _____

Address _____

Signature/s _____   _____

Bank sorting code number	For account of and account number	Amount		Total amount for each bank	
	Totals carried forward £				

2121

F16

PETTY CASH ACCOUNT

Dr												Cr
Received	Date	Fo	Details	V No	Total paid out							

F17

Petty Cash Voucher

Folio_____

Date_____19

For what required	AMOUNT	
	£	p

Signature_____

Passed by_____ _____

Petty Cash Voucher

Folio_____

Date_____19

For what required	AMOUNT	
	£	p

Signature_____

Passed by_____ _____

F18

PAY ADVICE

Name		Works No.

Week No.	Date	Code No.

£

Earnings: basic

      overtime

      bonus

      back pay

      other

Total Gross pay

Less pension

Gross pay for tax purposes

Less deductions: £

   Income Tax

   National Insurance

   Savings

   Social Club

   Other

Total deductions

NET PAY

F19

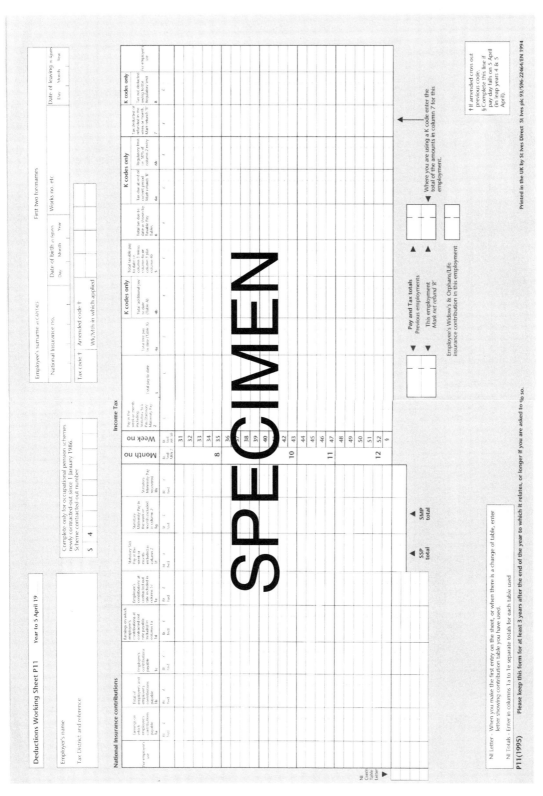

F20

149

PAYROLL

Week No:

Date:

Employee	GROSS PAY	National Insurance			Deductions			NET PAY
		Total employer's and employee's contbn.	Employer's contbn.	Employee's NI contbn.	Income tax payable	Other deductions	Total	
TOTALS								

F21

PERSONNEL RECORD CARD

Address	Next of kin
	Name:
	Address:
Telephone number	Date of birth
Date commenced	Marital status
Occupation	Full or part time
Salary	Tax code
Date Left	Reason for leaving
Previous employer	
Surname	Other names Department

F22

REMITTANCES BOOK

Date	Remitter's name	Method of payment	Account No	Amount £	Cashier's signature

F23

ACCIDENT REPORT FORM

Report of an accident or injury to a person at work or on duty and/or a dangerous occurrence.

This form must be completed in all cases of accident, injury or dangerous occurrence and submitted to the Safety Officer.

Injured person's:

Surname   Forenames

Title *Mr/Mrs/Miss/other (state)   Date of birth

Home address

Position held
*Employee/Student/Contractor/Visitor

Date and time of accident

Particulars of injury/incapacity

Activity at time of accident/injury

Place of accident/injury

Give full details of the accident and any injury suffered and explain how it happened

What first-aid treatment was given?

Was the injured person taken to hospital? If so, where?

State names and positions of any persons who were present when the accident occurred.

Signature of person reporting incident _____

Date of report _____
*Delete those which are inapplicable

F24

CIRCULATION SLIP		
Name	Initials	Date
1		
2		
3		
4		
5		
6		
Please circulate the attached document quickly		

F25

STOCK REQUISITION

No ....

Date ....

Quantity	Description	Stock Ref No	Section

Signed .... Storekeeper's initials

Authorised ....

F26

EMPLOYEE EXPENSES CLAIM

Name:

Bank Code:

Employee No.

Bank account No.

Departmental Code:

Date	Particulars	Car Mileage	Public Transport	Car Hire	Hotel accommodation	Meals	Sundries	Total	VAT Recoverable
	Total Mileage					Mileage Amount			
						TOTAL AMOUNT DUE			

These expenses have been wholly, exclusively and necessarily incurred on authorised business

Signed _____

Authorised   Date

F27

CLAIM FOR EXPENSES

Claimant's Name _____   Department _____

Date	Particulars of Travel	Car Engine cc Miles	Rail/ Air* £	Hotel Acc'dtn* £	Meals* £	Others* eg Taxis £	Daily Totals £
	Total mileage miles @ per mile						
	*Bills and receipts should be attached Please specify other expenses overleaf					Grand total	£

Authorised
and
Checked
by

Date _____

F28

CASH RECEIPT

From:

No:

Date _____ 19—

Description	£	
TOTAL		

RECEIVED WITH THANKS

From:

Cashier

VAT Registration No.

F29

157

DESK DIARY

Date:

Day:

Time:	Details	Venue
0900		
1000		
1100		
1200		
1300		
1400		
1500		
1600		
1700		
1800		
1900		
2000		
Notes:		

F30

Memo

To

From

Date

Subject

F31

MESSAGE FOR

M _____

WHILE YOU WERE OUT

M _____

Of _____

Telephone No: _____

Telephoned		Please ring	
Called to see you		Will call again	
Wants to see you		Urgent	

Message: _____

_____

_____

_____

_____

_____

_____

_____

_____

_____

Date_____   Time _____

Received by _____

F32

160

Date ....

Draft Telex Message

Telex number to be called ....

Answerback code ....

Message for: Name of person ....

Name of firm ....

Message:

Message drafted by: ....

Department ....

F33

161

RECEPTION APPOINTMENTS BOOK

Date:

Day:

Time	Visitor's name	Company	Appointment for	Venue

F34

162

Reception Register

Date	Time	Name of caller	Company	To see	Seen by	Department

F35

Certificate
of Posting

This is a receipt for ordinary letters. Keep it
safely to produce in the event of a claim.
The ordinary post should not be used for
sending money or valuable items.

Royal Mail

Please write the name, address and
postcode for each item you're sending
in the column below (in ink).

number of items   Officer's initials   date stamp

name   address and postcode

please continue on the back (*if necessary*)   P326 Feb 92

F36

164

Guaranteed Delivery

Affix the label above to the front of your letter/packet

Guaranteed Delivery Date

XX 3723 9454 9GB

XX 3723 9454 9GB
XX 3723 9454 9GB

After completion affix this label to the back of your letter/packet.

Sender's Name

Address

Postcode

PO Counter Reference **SP 3723 9454 9GB**

Customer Reference **SP 3723 9454 9GB**

Date Stamp

SP 3723 9454 9GB

Guaranteed Delivery Date

Officer's Signature

Sent To

Address

Postcode

Special Delivery
for a guaranteed delivery

F37

PARCEL ★ FORCE
Standard

Despatch Certificate

Fill in below, in ink, the name and address as written on each parcel and present them in the order listed. If using Trakback, write in column 1 the Customer Reference (bar code) number against each parcel. For information on compensation limits and exclusions, see overleaf. *An additional fee is payable if higher than normal compensation cover is required. See overleaf for details.* * This certificate is not required for Cash on Delivery parcels which have their own documentation.

Received _____ parcels as listed below

	1 Trakback Number (see over for details)	2 Name and Address (as written on parcel)	3 Postcode	Compensation Cover* Fee payable (tick if required)		
				£20	£150	£500
1				NO FEE		
2				NO FEE		
3				NO FEE		
4				NO FEE		
5				NO FEE		

Stamps for Compensation Fee
(to be cancelled by accepting officer)

Date stamp

PLEASE KEEP THIS CERTIFICATE SAFE, IT MUST BE PRODUCED IN THE EVENT OF A CLAIM

For retention by Post Office Counters

	£150	£500
Number of fees collected		

Date stamp

F38

Recorded

Royal Mail

Affix the label above to the front of your letter/packet

DY 6837 6919 7GB

DY 6837 6919 7GB

After completion affix this label to the
back of your letter/packet.

| Sender's Name |
| Address |
| Postcode |

| Customer Reference | DY 6837 6919 7GB | Customer Reference | DY 6837 6919 7GB |

Date Stamp		Sent To
		Address
Officer's Signature		Postcode

DY 6837 6919 7GB

Recorded
for a signature on delivery

Royal Mail

F39

F40